MELODRAMATIC UNIVERSE

A RIDE THROUGH THE KNOWN UNIVERSE

KOMAL SINGH

Dedicated to my loving sister, who inspired me to pursue my callings.

Contents

Preface *vii*

1. Your Place In Universe 1
2. Are You An Astronomer? 5
3. Naked Eye Observation 14
4. Cycles In The Sky 28
5. Moon Phases 38
6. Eclipses 48
7. Telescopes 59
8. The Gravity Of The Situation 71
9. Our Solar System 81
10. The Sun 91
11. The Earth 102
12. The Moon 114
13. The Mercury 127
14. The Venus 140
15. The Mars 150
16. The Jupiter 159
17. The Jupiter's Moons 169
18. The Saturn 184
19. The Uranus And The Neptune 198
20. The Asteroid Belt 210
21. The Comets 224
22. The Oort Cloud 234
23. The Meteor 246

Preface

This book focuses on astronomy and not astrology so we'll get into actual scientific information rather than who you're most compatible with and what the full moon means for your career. We'll start off with moon phases, eclipses and other things we can observe with the naked eye but then we'll expand out looking at the planets and non planets in our solar system ,extending our way till the Oort Cloud.

Astronomy may seem overwhelming because it's basically studying the biggest thing there is ,it's the science of everything in the freaking physical universe but that's what this book is for ,to break it down to you , learning about our universe and how it works, it is more than just Black holes and star clusters , it's about understanding how science and technology allows us to study the world around us and rethink our place in it . It's about finding out where we came from and weather there's other life , even other universes out there ,it's about expanding our understanding of ourselves and importantly our limits.

CHAPTER ONE

YOUR PLACE IN UNIVERSE

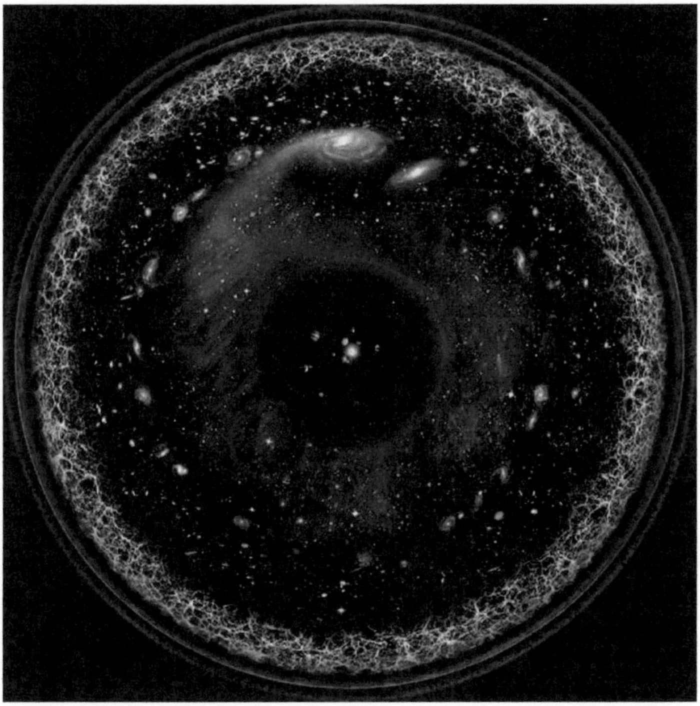

The Cosmos

As an enthusiast we might explore planets, stars, black holes, galaxies, subatomic particles and even the eventual fate of the universe itself but before we step into that let's take a step back, and talk about science. There are lots of definitions of science, one of them being...

> "*Science is the pursuit and application of knowledge and understanding of natural and social world following a systematic methodology based on evidence* ."

Its a body of knowledge, and a method of how we learned that knowledge.Science tells us that the stuff we think we know may not be perfectly known, it may be partly or entirely wrong, we need to watch the universe, see how it behaves, make guesses about why it's doing what it is doing and then try to think of ways to support or disprove those ideas.

Understanding that our understanding might be wrong is essential ,and trying to figure out the ways we may be mistaken is the only way the science can help us find our way to the truth...or at least the nearest approximation to that truth.

While learning science we may deviate from our paths a bit, but in the long run we get closer and closer to understanding reality and that is the strength of science and it's all around us ,whether you know it or not you're soaking in science. You're a mammal, you have mass, mitochondria in your cells are generating energy , you are breathing oxygen, throwing out carbon dioxide.But astronomy works differently it's still science but astronomy puts you in your place.

Because of astronomy we know we are standing on a sphere of mostly molten rock and metal,13,000 km across with an atmosphere about a 100 kms high surrounded by a magnetic field that protects us from the onslaught of sub atomic particles from the sun 150,000,000 km away which is also flooding space with light that reaches across space to illuminate the planets past the Kuiper Belt, through the Oort cloud into interstellar space, past the nearest stars,which orbit along with gas clouds and dust lanes in a gigantic spiral galaxy we call the Milky Way. That has a super massive black hole in its centre and is surrounded by 150 globular clusters and a halo of dark matter and dwarf galaxies, all of which can be seen by other galaxies in our local group like Andromeda and Triangulum, and our group is on the outskirts of the Virgo galaxy cluster which is part of the Virgo Supercluster, which is just one of the many other gigantic structures that stretch most of the way across the visible universe,which is 90 billion light years across and expanding every day , even faster today than yesterday due to mysterious dark energy, and even that might be part of an infinitely larger multiverse that extends forever both in space and time .

See? astronomy puts you in your place.

Our Galaxy

CHAPTER TWO

ARE YOU AN ASTRONOMER?

The Ancient Astronomer

You have this book in your hand, you have the jest to know about this vast universe , does your shear curiosity make you an astronomer?

But who exactly is an astronomer?

Astronomers look through telescopes for a living, study the data that comes from the detectors attached to them . Some may work as programmers, programming telescopes, coding and calibrating the camera to be used by an astronaut. Once the data from the camera are taken and analyzed, the astronomer has to know what to do with them and do the observations with the physical models of how stars blow up or how galaxies form, or the way gas flows through space.

They are well versed with mathematics and physics because that's how they test their hypothesis .And someone who does that is generally called an astrophysicists.

Of course those telescopes and detectors don't create themselves ,engineers are needed to design and build them and technicians to use them . Most astronomers don't actually use the telescopes themselves anymore, someone who is trained in their specific use does that for them. Some of those instruments go into outer space and some go to the other terrestrial objects like the moon and Mars .

We need astronomers and engineers and software programmers who can build those too and then at the end of all this we need people to tell you all about it teachers ,professors, writers, bloggers, even artist .

So if you have an interest in the universe,if you love to look up at the stars if you crave to understand what's going on literally over your head then who am I to say you're not an astronomer .

Hipparchus, Ancient Greek Astronomer

However you define astronomy, humans have been looking up at the sky for as long as we have been human.

Certainly ancient people noticed the big shiny ball (the Sun) in the sky and how it brightened every place while it was up,and how it got dark when it was gone.The other fainter shiny ball (the Moon)wasn't quite as good at lighting up the night. They probably took that sort of thing pretty seriously,they probably also noticed that when certain stars appeared in the sky the weather started getting warmer and the days longer. And when other stars were seen the weather would get colder and daytime shorter. And when humans settled down discovered agriculture and started farming no two single patterns in the sky would've had an even greater impact. It told them when to plant seeds and when to harvest.

The cycles in the sky became pretty important,so important that it wasn't hard to imagine gods up there looking down at us weak humans interfering with our lives. Surely if the stars tell us when to plant and control the weather ,seasons and the length of the day ,they control our lives too.Thats when astrology was born.

Ancient Astrology

Astrology literally means the study of the stars ,as a word it's been used before science became a formal method of studying nature. On the other hand astronomy means study of the law of the stars.

otherwise invisible to us , details of galaxies, beautiful clouds of gas and dust in space .

And then in the latter half of the last century digital detectors were invented which were even more sensitive than film. We could use computers to directly analyze observations and our knowledge leaped again. When these were coupled with telescopes sent into orbit around the earth where our boiling atmosphere doesn't blur out observations we began yet another revolution.

And where are we now?

We'vecome such a long way that we can ask questions that our ancestors would not have dared.

We take the idea of looking for life on alien planet seriously and spend billions doing it .

Our Galaxy is one of 100 billion others we can only directly see 4 percent of the universe.Still we dare make an attempt to explore it.

Stars explode and when they do they create the stuff of life the, iron in our blood calcium in our bones ,the phosphorus that is the backbone of our DNA.The most common kind a star in the universe is so faint you can't even see it without a telescope

Our solar system is overflowing with worlds more bizarre than we could have dreamed . Nature has more imagination,it comes up with some weird stuff. But we are clever too, we big brained apes.We'velearned a lot but there is still a long way to go.

An extremely large telescope ,using lasers

TMT Observatory

CHAPTER THREE

NAKED EYE OBSERVATION

Milky Way Galaxy

In astronomy naked eye refers to “no binoculars , no telescope” .

Just you, your eyeballs, and a nice dark site to view the heaven above.That’s how we did astronomy for thousands of years. It is actually pretty amazing what you can figure out about the universe just by looking at it.

Imagine yourself somewhere far away from City lights, where you have an unobstructed view of the cloudless sky. The sun sets, and for a few minutes you just watch as the sky darkens ,then you notice a star appear in the east just over a tree ,then another , and another ,within an hour or so you are standing beneath an incredible display, a sky full of stars.

What do you notice right away?

A Sky Full Of Stars

First there are a lot of stars, a person with normal vision can see a few thousand stars at any given time, there are roughly 6000 to 10,000 stars in total that are bright enough to be detected by eye alone, depending on how good your eyesight is .

Next thing you'll notice is that they are not all the same brightness. A handful are very bright, a few more are a bit fainter but still pretty bright, and so on. The faintest star you can see are the most abundant, vastly outnumbering the bright ones. This is due to the combination of two effects . One is that not all stars have the same intrinsic, physical brightness. Some are dim bulbs while others are monsters, blasting out as much light in one second as the sun does in a day.

The second factor is that not all starsare at the same distance from us. The farther away a star is the fainter it is. Interestingly ,out of the two dozen or so brightest satrs in the sky , half are bright because they are close to earth, and half are much farther away but incredibly luminous, so they still appear bright to us.

This is a running theme in astronomy and science in general .Some effects you see have more than one cause. Things are not always as simple as they seem.

The ancient Greek astronomer Hipparchus is generally credited for creating the first catalog of stars ranking them by brightness.

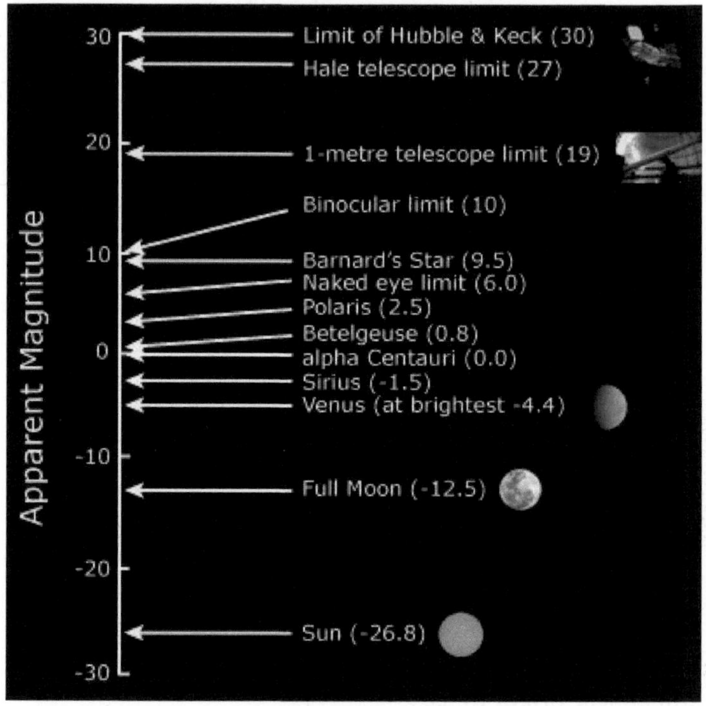

Brightness of Stars

He came up with a system called magnitudes ,where the brightest stars were 1st magnitude, the next brightest were 2nd magnitude , down to 6th magnitude. We still use a variation of this system today, thousands of years later. The faintest stars ever seen using Hubble space telescope are about magnitude 31. The fainteststars you can see with your eyes is about 10 billion times brighter .

Sirius

The brightest star in the night sky called Sirius , the dog star, is about 1000 times brighter than the faintest star you can see. Let's take a look at some of those bright stars, like , Vega. It looks blue. And Betelgeuse looks red. Arcturus is orange , Capella yellow. Are those stars really of those colours? By eye, only the brightest stars seem to have colour, while the fainter ones all just look white. That's because the colour receptors in your eye aren't very light sensitive, and only the brightest stars can trigger them.

Another thing you'll notice is that stars aren't scattered evenly in the sky they form patterns and shapes. This is mostly coincidence, but we humans are pattern recognizing animals so it's totally understandable that ancient astronomers divided the skies up into constellations and named them after familiar objects.

Orion

Orion is probably the most famous constellation, it really does look like a person, arms raised up , and most civilizations saw it that way.

There's also Delphinus, its only five stars, but it's easy to see it as a dolphin jumping out of water.

And scorpius , which isn't hard to imagine as the venomous arthropod.

Others , well not so much

Pisces , is a fish. Cancer is a crab ,only if you look closely.

Although they were rather arbitrarily defined in ancient times , today we recognize 88 official constellations, and their boundaries are carefully marked on the sky. When we say a star is in the constellation of Ophiuchus, it's because the location of the star puts it inside that constellation's boundaries.

Ursa Major

Not every group of stars makes a constellation , like The Big Dipper , is only one part of constellation of Ursa Major, The Big Bear.

Most of the brightest stars have proper names , usually Arabic.

Delphinus

During the dark ages, it was the Persian astronomer Adb al Rahman al sufi who translated ancient Greek astronomy texts into Arabic,and those name were stuck with us since then . However there are a lot more stars than there are proper names , so astronomers use designations for them. The stars in any constellation are given Greek letters in order of their brightness, so we have alpha orion , the brightest star in orion, then beta and so on. One may run out of letters, hence most modern catalogs use numbers.

EVER HEARD OF LIGHT POLLUTION?

Light pollution is a serious problem for astronomers, here the lights get blasted up into the sky instead of towards the ground

This lights up the sky making fainter objects much difficult to see.

That's why observatories tend to be built in remote areas, as far from the cities as possible.

From within a big city it is impossible to see the milky way,the faint glowy streak across the sky, that's actually the combined light of billions of stars.

It gets washed out with even mild light pollution .

Light pollution also affects the way nocturnal animals hunt, how insects breed,and more , by disrupting their normal daily cycles.

Level Of Pollution

Even if you don't have dark skies, there's another thing that you can notice when you look up. If you look carefully , you might see that a couple of the brightest stars look different than the others.They don't twinkle,that's because they aren't stars , they are planets

Twinkling happens because the air over our heads is turbulent, and as it blows past, it distorts the incoming light from stars, making them appearto slightly shift position and brightness several times per second.

But planets are much closer to us and appear bigger, so the distortion doesn'taffect them much.

There are five naked eye planets, Mercury , Venus, Mars , Jupiter, Saturn.

Uranus is right on the verge of visibility.

Venus is the third brightest natural object in the sky, after sun and moon.

Jupiter and mars are frequently brighter than the brightest stars, too.

If you stay outside for an hour or two, you'll notice that the stars move ,like the sky is a gigantic sphere wheeling around you over the course of the night. In factthat's how the ancient thought of it. If you could measure it , you would find the celestial sphere spins once every day. This is really just the reflection of earth'sspinning , of course. The earth rotates once a day and we are stuck to it. So it looks like the sky is spinning around us in the opposite direction. There's an interesting thing that happens because of this. Look at the spinning globe. It rotates on an axis that goes through the poles, and halfway between them is the equator. If you stand on the equator, you make a big circle around the center of the earth over a day.

But if you move north or south towards one pole or the other, that circle gets smaller. When you stand on the pole, you don't make a circle at all, you just spin around at a point. It's the same thing with the sky. As the sky spins over us, just like with the earth, it has two poles and an equator. A star on celestial equator makes a big circle around the sky, and stars to the north or south make smaller ones.

A star right on the celestial pole,would not move at all like it was nailed to that spot, all night long. And this is just what we see. Photographic time exposure shows it best. The motion of the stars show up a streak. The longer the exposure, the longer the streak, making a circular arc in sky. You can see stars near the celestial equator making big circles. And by coincidence, there's also a middling bright star that sits very close to the north celestial pole. That's called Polaris,the north star or pole star.

Polaris

Because of that, it doesn't appear to rise or set, and is always to the north, motionless. It really is coincidence , that there is no southern pole star, unless you count Sigma Octans,a dim bulb barely visible by eye that's not all that close to the south pole of the sky anyway. But even Polaris isn't exactly on the pole , its offset a little bit. So it does make a cicle in the sky, but one so small you'd never notice.

By eye, night after night,Polaris is the constant in the sky. Always there, never moving. Remember, the sky's motion is the reflection of the earth's motion, if you were standing on the north pole of earth, you'd see Polaris at the sky's zenith, that is straight overhead, fixed and unmoving. Stars on the celestial equator would appear to circle the horizon once per day. But this also means that stars south of the celestial equator can't be seen from the earth's north pole. They're always below the horizon. So this in turn means that which stars you see depends on where you are on earth.

Tilted Earth

At the north pole, you only see stars north of the celestial equator. At the earth's south pole , you only see stars south of the celestial equator. For Antarctica ,Polaris is forever hidden from the view. Standing on the earth's equator, you would see Polaris on the horizon to the north, and Sigma Octans to the horizon to the south, and over the course of the day the entire celestial sphere would spin around you. Amazing, right! You just have to stand there at a place to see the universe move around you and make the naked eye observation.

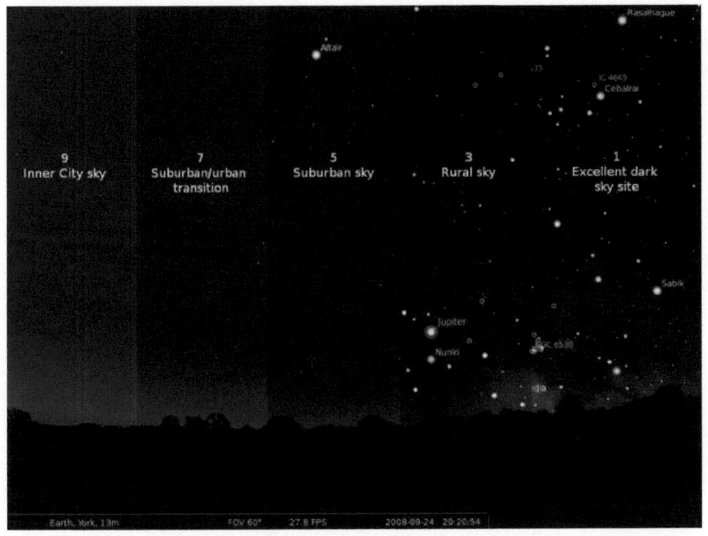

Light Pollution

CHAPTER FOUR

CYCLES IN THE SKY

Cycles in the sky

Under a dark sky ,you can see thousands of stars. If you watch for a few hours, you can see them rise and set as the earth rotates once a day.

If you go outside the next night at the same time you will see the things look pretty much the same as they did the night before .The stars rise and set ,Polaris hangs in the north and so on .

One day ,hardly makes any difference to the sky's appearance but what if you wait for another night or a week. If you are that patient and observant you can spot subtle changes in the sky.

Lets say a couple of weeks have passed . Remember that star that was just over a tree in the east when the sunset , the one that made you first notice the stars are rising and setting , go look at it again.

If you happen to be out at the same time you would expect that star to be in the same place but its not, it is actually a bit higher above the tree and if you look West ,stars that were well off the horizon just after sunset last week are now lower.

If you wait a month ,this effect is even more pronounced ,all new constellations will be visible in the sky after sunset. This is because the earth is going around the sun literally changing her viewpoint on the sky. The earth takes a year to orbit the sun once, everyday it moves a little bit along its orbit and as it does, from the earth's perspective distant stars appear to move their positions relative to the sun so one day we might see a start very near the sun, but the next day the angle is a bit bigger.

At some point about six months after we first saw it, the star is the directly opposite the sun in the sky. Then the angle starts to shrink again as the start approaches the sun from the opposite side until after a full year,the cycle repeats .

A repeating cycle

What this means to you is that the stars appear to rise and set at different times over the course of the year.

Stars in the east rise about four minutes earlier every night and stars in the West set four minutes earlier.

A Constellation that was entirely below the eastern horizon at sunset one month might be completely visible after sunset the next month .

Another way to think about it is that the stars appear to be fixed and as the earth circles the sun ,the sun moves through the stars over the course of the year making a complete circle around the sky once per year.

The path it takes is a reflection of the earth's path around the sun ,a line in the sky,we call that line ecliptic.

That means the sun passes through the same constellations in the sky every year every year. We give those constellations a special name ,the zodiac. Every year during a given month the Sun will appear to be in a certain zodiacal constellationfrom Sagittarius through Scorpius ,Libra ,Virgo ,Leo ,Cancer and the rest.

Eventually over the year, the sun returns to Sagittarius and the cycle starts again .

But even though we talk about this process in terms of the sun's movement. It is really the path travelled by the earth that creates this affect as our perspective moves with it.

And of course the planets move in the sky as well mercury Venus Mars ,they orbit the sun too and they do so in approximately the same plane the earth does.If you could can see the solar system from the side it would look flat so do us ,on earth the planet's go around the sky over the course of a year and they also appear to change their positions relative to the sun and the stars .

The inner planets mercury and Venus move so rapidly you can see their motion after a single night. The outer planets are more leisurely ,but wait long enough and they too will be seen to move, sliding through the constellations.

By the way the word planet is greek for "wanderer".

There's another aspect of all this you might notice over time. You've probably seen a globe and noticed that the axis of it is tilted that is it's not straight up and down, perpendicular to how it sits. That's because a globe is a modeling the earth and the earth is tilted.

Tilted axis of the earth

The earth spins on its axis once per day and orbits the sun once per year but earth's axis is tilted with respect to its orbital plane by 23.5° and this has a profound effect on our planet.

Imagine for a moment that the earth's axis were exactly perpendicular to its orbit straight up and down if that were the case every day the sun would take the same path across the sky if you were on the equator the sun would rise go exactly overhead and set. If you were on the pole the sun would appear to go around the horizon every day neither rising nor setting it would always be twilight, but that's not the case. The earth is tilted.

In the months of June and July,the earth's north pole is tipped towards the sun. Six months later it's pointed away. This affects the path sun takes across the sky. Instead of it taking the same path every day in the northern summer when we're tipped towards the sun, the sun takes a higher path in the sky because the path is longer, the days are longer too.

Six months later in December and January ,the earth's pole is tipped away, the sun takes a lower path in the sky and because the path is shorter the days are shorter too.

That's why we have seasons. When the sun is up high in the sky it shines straight down on the ground heating it better and days are longer so it has more time to heat us.

In the winter it's the reverse the sun is lower so it can't warm us up that efficiently and it has less time to do so.

There you go ..season.

The earth'saxis is tipped . If it weren't the seasons wouldn't occur and the temperature of the Earth wouldn't change month to month.

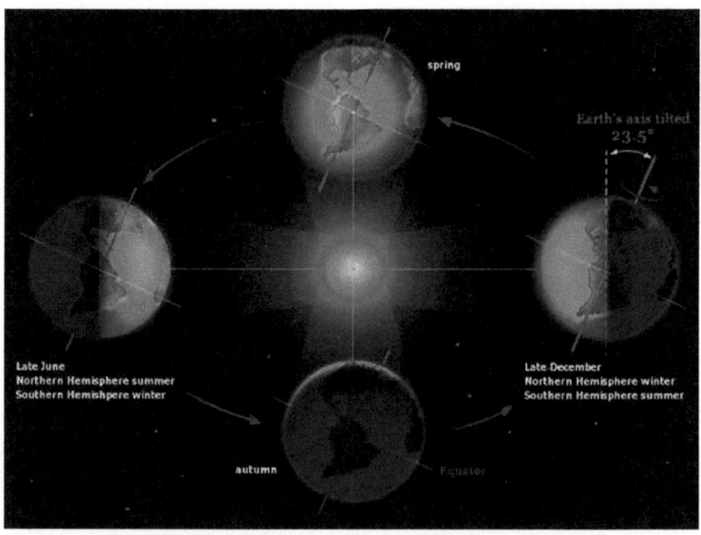

Seasons from space

There is a common misconception that the earth has seasons because it orbits the sun on an ellipse,and so it's closer to the sun in summer and farther in winter.

Whileits true the orbit is elliptical, earth is closer to the sun in January on the order of 5 million km or so than it is in july. It's the angle of the sun's rays that makes winter cold and summer hot not our distance from the sun.

Also you may know that when it's summer in the northern hemisphere it's winter in the southern when the North Pole is tipped towards the sun, the south pole is tipped away. so northern and southern hemisphere seasons are opposite to each other.

But nothing in astronomy is permanent the North Pole is not always going to point towards the sun in June and Polaris is not always going to be the North Star.That's because our planet's axis is actually moving .

Have you ever seen a spinning top start to wobble its axis, moving in a slow circle even as the top itself spins this is called procession . And the earth does it too.

Our planet spins on its axis once per day,but the axis wobbles ,making a very slow circle that takes26,000 years to complete.

This affects a lot of what we see in the sky for example Polaris wont always be the pole star.

Every year the poll points a little farther from that star making a big circle 47° across. For ancient Egyptians, the star Thuban was the pole star, and about 11,000 years that position will be held by the bright star Vega.

Also the date the sun is in a particular zodiac constellation changes slowly due to the procession as well. When the ancients first thought of this idea ,the sun was in Aries on March 22 the vernal equinox(first day of spring) but due to precession it's now in Pisces. that's why your astrological sign doesn't match where the sun actually is.

In the sky 2000 years of recession has changed them .One of the many reasons astrology is silly.

It's incredible to think about the earth, the sun the stars ,they allow was to tell the time and time of the year just by looking up and paying attention. This is why the stars were so important to ancient humans .

The stars were like a clock and a calendar in the sky long before we had invented either. We've actually learnt a lot about sky just by looking at it. of course ,some of the stuff explained we've learned through other means like the earth spinning , stars have different intrinsic brightness and so on but all that knowledge and far more got its start by people who went outside and looked up.

Later as we applied maths and physics to what we observed, we learned even more,and could then go back and explain what we saw.

So don't discount naked eyes astronomy it's all we had for thousands of years.

In fact I think we lost something when we started using clocks and calendars and moving to cities with bright lights that washed away the stars from the sky.

Those folks long ago were tied to the sky they knew it like you know the street in your neighborhood .They could see the stars rise and said they knew the glory of the Milky Way sprawled across the heavens, even if they didn't know exactly what it was. We do know now with our knowledge gained over the centuries but it comes at the cost of losing touch with the sky .

The universe belongs to everyone go outside and if you can *soak up your share* .

A beautiful night sky

CHAPTER FIVE

MOON PHASES

Moon Phases

Besides the Sun, the Moon is the most obvious object in the sky.

Bright, silvery, with tantalizing features on its face, it's been the target of imagination, poetry, science,and even the occasional rocket.If you pay even the most cursory attention to it, you'll see that it changes everyday; sometimes it's up in the day, sometimes at night, and its shape is always changing.

What causes this behavior?

The Moon is basically a giant ball of rock 3500 kilometers across hanging in space. Itssurface is actually pretty dark, with about the same reflectivity as a chalkboard or asphalt.

However, it looks bright to us because it's sitting in full sunlight; the Sun illuminatesit, and it reflects that light down to us here on Earth.

And because it's a sphere, and orbiting the Earth, the way we see it lit by the Sunchanges with time.

That's what causes its phases.

The important thing to remember through all this is, because the Moon is a ball and inspace, half of it is always illuminated by the Sun!

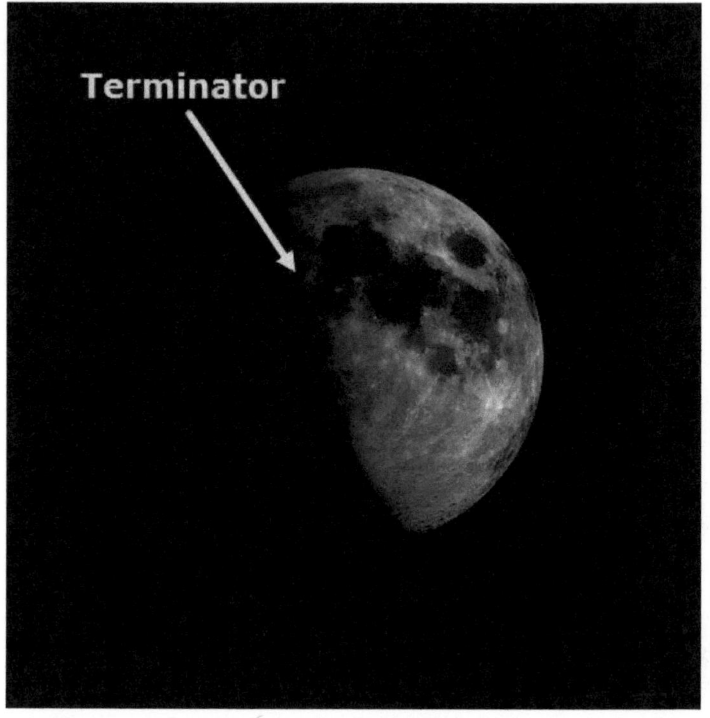

Terminator

This is true for the Earth, too, and every spherical object in space; half faces theSun, half faces away. We call the part facing the Sun the daylight or bright side, and the half facing away the night or dark side.

The phase of the Moon refers to what shape the Moon appears to us; how much of it wesee illuminated from the Earth. The key to all this is this line, dividing the lit dayside from the unlit night side. We call that line the terminator.

If you're facing the moon, with the sun behind you, you're seeing the half of themoon that is fully illuminated by sunlight and it looks full. If you're off to theside you see half of the lit side and half of the dark side and we say the moon is halffull. If the sun is on the other side of the moon, you're look at the unlit half, andit looks dark. Now, here we haven't moved anything except our point of view here,so at all times the Moon is always half lit, and half dark. Remember that.

The phase of the Moon we see depends on from what direction the sunlight's hitting it,and the angle we see that from Earth.

The Moon orbits the Earth roughly once per month. In fact, that's where the word "month"comes from; "month" and "Moon" are cognates, words that have similar etymologicalhistories, and in most languages, including English, the two words are very similar. The length of time we call the month is derived from the length of time it takes the Moonto go through all its phases -- 29.5 days.

So to describe the phases, let's start at the beginning: New Moon.

New Moon happens when the Sun, Moon, and Earth are all more or less in a line. The Moon'sorbit is actually tipped a bit to the Earth's, so sometimes new Moon happens when the Moonis "below" the Sun, or "above" it. But at some point in its orbit, at some pointin the month, it appears to be as close to the Sun as it can.

Moon Phases

What does this look like from Earth?

The Moon is between the Earth and Sun, so from our perspective we only see the darkhalf, the unilluminated half, of the Moon. The other side, the far side, of the Moonis lit, but we can't see it. It makes sense then to call this the beginning of the Moon'scycle, hence the term "New Moon".

Now think about this for a sec: Because the Moon is near the Sun in the sky, it travelsacross the sky with the Sun. It's up during the day! You can only see it from the part of the Earth that's lit, which is when it's daytime. It's a very common misconceptionthat the Moon is only up at night, but it's up during the day literally just as often.

At New Moon, the Moon stays near the Sun, so it rises at sunrise, and sets at sunset.

This makes it extremely difficult to see; it is, after all, sitting next to the brightestobject in the sky, and only a little bit of it is lit from our perspective.

But not for long. Because the Moon is orbiting the Earth, after a couple of days it's moveda bit to the east. Now we're seeing it along a slight angle, and we can see a little bitof the illuminated half of the Moon on its side toward the Sun.

The terminator, the day/night line, appears curved around the Moon, so what we see isa thin illuminated crescent Moon. At this point the crescent is still very thin, with the horns of the crescent pointing away from the Sun.

Note that the Moon is still pretty close to the Sun in the sky, just a bit to the east,rising maybe an hour or two after sunrise. But this means it's up all day, and then

sets after the Sun does. This is the best time to see the crescent Moon, when the Sunhas already set and the sky starts to get dark. The Moon will be low over the westernhorizon, and it will set soon after the Sun does.

Let's wait a couple of days.

OK, now the Moon has moved a bit more in its orbit around the Earth, and is farther fromthe Sun in the sky. We see a little more of the illuminated part, and the crescent iswider. Since it's getting thicker, we say this is a "waxing crescent" Moon; waxingmeans growing or getting bigger. It's also well away from the Sun now, so it's easier to spot, even during the day before sunset.

Seven or so days after new Moon we get to our first milestone: the Moon is now one-quarterof the way around its orbit. It's 90° away from the Sun in the sky, which means we'relooking straight down on the terminator, the Moon's day/night line. It cuts right down the middle of the visible face of the Moon, so it's half lit, with the sunward sideof the Moon visible and the other side dark.

Confusingly, this phase is properly named "first quarter" because the Moon is ¼of the way through its cycle, ¼ of the way through its orbit around the Earth, even thoughit looks half full. So it's not really the half-full moon -- astronomers prefer "firstquarter," so if you want to sound all astronomery, then you should call it that.

But time marches on. The Moon continues on its gravitational dance with Earth, swingingaround its orbit. Now more than half full, we say its shape is "gibbous", which meansswollen or convex. Since it's getting wider, this is actually the waxing gibbous phase of the Moon. It rises in the late afternoon, and is up most of the night.

Our next big step comes two weeks after new Moon, when it's moved halfway through itsorbit. It is now opposite the Sun in the sky, 180° around. The Earth is between the Moonand Sun, so we're looking at the fully-illuminated half of the Moon. This is the full Moon.

Moon Phases

Because it's opposite the Sun, it rises at sunset and sets and sunrise; it's upall night shining down on the Earth.

But again, wait a couple of days and things change. When the Moon is full it's 180°around the sky from the Sun, so as it continues to move around the Earth in a circle the distancebetween it and the Sun is now starting to decrease, even as it continues on in the samedirection. As before, it keeps rising and setting later, but now it rises after sunset,and sets after sunrise. If you get up early in the morning as the Sun is just rising inthe east, you'll see the nearly-but-not-quite full Moon setting in the west.

Not only that, but we're about to go through all the phases again, but in reverse order.

A few days after full Moon the lit side is shrinking. It's in the waning, or shrinking,gibbous phase.

Then, three weeks or so after new Moon, and a week after full, the Moon is once againhalf lit, the terminator splitting the Moon's face in two even halves. This is the "thirdquarter" Moon, because the Moon is ¾ of the way through its cycle. It's a lot likethe first quarter, but the side that was lit is now dark, and vice versa. It's 270°around the sky from the Sun. It rises at midnight and sets at noon.

A few days later and the Moon is a crescent again, getting thinner. It's now a "waningcrescent." It rises just a couple of hours before sunrise, and sets a couple of hours before sunset.

Then, finally, we're back where we started. One month after new Moon, the Moon has traveled360° around the sky, and is once again as close to the Sun as it can get. It's newMoon, and the cycle starts up again as it has for time immemorial.

An interesting thing happens if you move your perspective from the Earth to the Moon. Thephases of the Moon we see from Earth depend on the angle of the Moon and Sun in the sky.

But on the Moon, the angles are exactly 180° reversed; at new Moon, when theMoon is between the Earth and Sun, the Earth is opposite the Sun as seen from the Moon.

It's full Earth!

All the other phases are opposite too, so when we see a full Moon, a Moon-dweller wouldsee a new Earth, and so on.

Have you ever looked at the thin crescent Moon and seen the ghostly face of the restof the unlit side? That's because it's not really unlit: the nearly full Earth isreflecting sunlight on the Moon, lighting up the otherwise dark part.

The Earth is bigger and more reflective than the Moon, so it's actually 50 times brighterthan a full Moon! This glow is called Earthshine, a term I quite like. Even more poetically,it's been called "the old Moon in the new Moon's arms", referring to the unlitpart surrounded by the crescent new Moon's horns.

Crescent Moon

That's lovely, isn't it?

The Moon is one of the most beautiful and most gratifying objects in the sky to observe.

It's different every day! Yet it's also the same, because we see, more or less, thesame half of it, the same face all the time. It's big and bright, and the features onits surface discernible by eye (and even better with binoculars or a small telescope).

As the phases change, inexorably, day after day, the angle of sunlight hitting the surfacechanges, bringing new things into our view. The motions become comforting, even familiar.

It's a reminder that the Universe may seem strange and complicated and forbidding atfirst, but over time, as you get outside and experience it, it becomes your neighbourhood.

Welcome home.

CHAPTER SIX

ECLIPSES

Eclipse

We humans of planet Earth benefit from a great coincidence. It's a coincidence of time,and of space. And of math.

The coincidence is this: the Sun is about 400 times wider than the Moon, and it'salso on average about 400 times farther away than the Moon.

The apparent size of an object in the sky depends on how big it is and how far awayit is... so these numbers being equal means the Sun and the Moon appear to be about thesame size in the sky.

And that's where another interesting thing comes in: Sometimes, the Moon passes directlybetween the Earth and the Sun. It doesn't happen all that often, but when it does, you get magic.

Or even better: You get SCIENCE.

You get an eclipse.

An eclipse is a generic term in astronomy for when one object passes into the shadowof another object, darkening or blocking it.

A solar eclipse is when the Moon blocks the Sun, casting a shadow on the Earth, and alunar eclipse is when the Earth blocks the Sun, casting a shadow on the Moon.

Solar Eclipse

But how do they work?

Well, the Moon orbits the Earth once per month, and the Earth orbits the Sun once per year.

If the Moon's orbit were perfectly aligned with the Earth's, essentially sharing thesame plane, we'd get a solar eclipse every new Moon and a lunar eclipse every full Moon!

But we don't. That's because the Moon's orbit is tilted with respect to Earth's,by about 5°.

What that means is that, at new Moon, the Moon can be as much as 5° away from the Sun,passing "above" or "below" the Sun in the sky, thereby missing it, from our perspective.

But sometimes the Moon is in the right place at the right time, and at new Moon, it liesperfectly in line between the Sun and the Earth. And when that happens, we get a solareclipse. This geometry happens at least twice per year, and sometimes as much as five times per year.

Lunar Eclipse

What's happening physically in space is that the Moon is casting a long shadow. Usuallythat shadow misses the Earth, but during an eclipse the Moon's shadow falls on the Earth's surface.

In fact, there are two shadows from the Moon, one inside the other. One is a narrow cone,tapering to a point away from the Moon. If you're anywhere physically inside this cone,the Moon appears big enough to completely block the Sun. That means this shadow is verydark, and we call it the umbra (which is Latin for – you guessed it – "shadow".

Outside of this deep umbral shadow is a wider conical region where, if you're in it, theSun is only partially blocked; you can still see some of the Sun past the Moon.

You'regetting less light, and so you're technically shadowed, but it's not quite as dark asthe umbra. This region is called the "penumbra"; "pen" in this case for Latin meaning "almost," or "nearly."

When the umbra touches the Earth, we get a total solar eclipse. But what does that look like from the ground?

You don't get a total eclipse right away. First, the edge of the Moon slips in frontof the Sun, and we see a little dip in the Sun's limb, its edge as seen from Earth(that's the start of the penumbra sweeping over you).

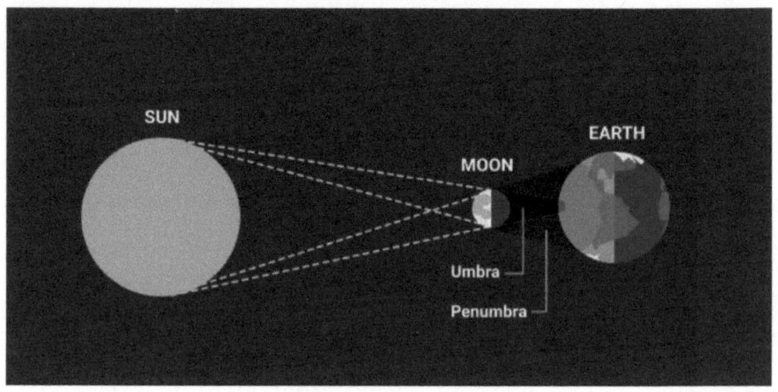

Umbra and Penumbra

As the Moon slowly moves, that dip grows, becoming a bite. The Sun becomes a thick crescent,then a thin one.

As the Sun becomes an ever-thinner crescent, the sky begins to darken. Then, finally, theMoon's black disk completely covers the Sun — the umbra sweeps over your location.

And at that moment, totality begins.

You might think that this just means the sky gets dark, and it's like night outside fora while. But a total eclipse is far more than that. And that's because of the Sun's corona.

The corona is the sun's atmosphere, an ethereally thin envelope of gas that stretches from the Sun's surface into space for millions of kilometers.

It's really faint, and therefore usually completely overwhelmed by the intensely brightlight from the Sun.

But when the Moon blocks the Sun's face, the corona becomes visible. It surrounds theSun, filaments and tendrils extending into the sky, an incredibly beautiful sight. Iknow many people who have said it's the most spectacular thing they have ever seen.

And there's more. The Moon's edge isn't smooth — there are craters and other depressions.

Craters right at the Moon's edge allow sunlight to stream past. We see these as bright patchesaround the eclipsed Sun, which are called Baily's Beads - because they were firstdescribed by English astronomer Francis Baily in 1836!

Baily's Beads

Because the Moon and Sun are very nearly the same apparent size, totality is brief.

The longest it can last is only about seven or eight minutes. That's how long it takesthe umbra to move over one spot on the Earth. When totality ends, and the Moon starts tomove off of the Sun's face, for a moment just a single spot of the Sun is unblocked,glowing fiercely on one side of the Moon. Sometimes you can get a circle of light aroundthe Moon's surface, and together with the bright spot it looks like a celestial wedding ring.

Diamond Ring Effect

In fact, this is called the Diamond Ring effect.

Then, inexorably, the Moon pulls away from the Sun, and the order of events is reversed.

The umbra is gone, but you're still in the penumbral shadow. The Sun shows a thin crescent,then a thick one, then a dip in its side... and then it's all over.

The umbral shadow of the Moon is pretty small where it hits the Earth, so a total eclipseis a local event. If you're too far north and south, you don't get a total eclipse,you only get a partial one. Which is still cool, but lacks the mystique of a total eclipse.

Remember too that the Moon's orbit around the Earth is an ellipse. That means sometimesit's closer to the Earth, and sometimes farther.

If a solar eclipse happens when the Moon is at the far end of its orbit, it can actuallybe smaller than the Sun in the sky. It doesn't block the entire face of the Sun, and it leaves a ring of light around the black circle of the Moon.

Annular Eclipse

This technical name for this shape is annulus, so this event is called an annular eclipse.

A lot of people think if you look at a total solar eclipse you can go permanently and completelyblind. That's really not true. But, some parts of eclipse-watching are more dangerous than others.

I mean, obviously it's not a good idea to stand there and stare at the sun. Lookingat even the uneclipsed Sun for more than a moment is painful, and that pain is the resultof the damage that solar radiation is doing to your retinas.

But when viewing an eclipse, the real concern is right after totality ends. During totalityit's dark, so your pupils have dilated to let more light in. But then there's theflash of sunlight when the Moon moves off, and that's intense enough to damage your retinas.

That's why astronomers recommend extreme caution when viewing an eclipse; because that

flash can catch you by surprise.

When viewing the Sun, don't just stand there and stare at it; you should always have eyeprotection. And make sure you have safety-approved filters; don't try the the home-made tricksyou might have heard of -- like looking through an old CD or DVD, or using old-style camerafilm as a filter.

These can let through too much infrared and ultraviolet light, and again can dilate yourpupils, actually making things worse.

Now, you don't have to worry about hurting your eyes at all when viewing a lunar eclipse.

Because, in that case, it's the Earth that blocks the Sun, and the Earth's shadow fallson the Moon.

So go nuts.

But one big difference between the two kinds of eclipses is who can see them.

A solar eclipse is localized to one spot on the Earth, or really a swath along the groundas the Moon's umbral shadow sweeps across the Earth's surface.

But a lunar eclipse is when the Moon moves into Earth's shadow, so anyone on Earthfacing the Moon can see a lunar eclipse.

The Earth has umbral and penumbral shadows, too. When the Moon first enters the Earth'spenumbra, the dimming is so slight you hardly notice it. But as the Moon moves deeper intothe penumbra, it starts to darken. Sometimes it changes color, turning a deep orange orblood red.

That's because the Earth is starting to block the sunlight heading toward the moon,and the only light that gets through is coming through the thickest part of our atmosphere.

This blocks blue and green light, leaving only red to come through.

That's why the Moon and Sun look red to us when they're on the horizon, rising andsetting, too. When you look upon the red eclipsed Moon, you're seeing the light from all thesunrises and sunsets in the world hitting the Moon and reflecting back to us.

Finally, the Moon starts to enter the Earth's umbra, and the real eclipse begins. At firstit looks like a bite is taken out of it — that curving arc is the shadow of the edge of theEarth! The Moon moves deeper and deeper into the shadow until it's completely darkened.

The Earth is bigger than the Moon, so the Earth's umbra is much wider; while a solareclipse is over in minutes, a total lunar eclipse can last nearly two hours.

There's not a lot of new science you can do with a lunar eclipse. But if you know alittle geometry, you can use the size and shape of the Earth's shadow on the Moon to get the relative sizes of the Earth and Moon.

Ancient Greeks did just this, and got a number that wasn't too far off. They also knewhow big the Earth was using other methods, and so they had a decent estimate for thesize of the Moon...nearly 2000 years before the invention of the telescope!

They also knew the shape of the Earth's shadow was always a circle, which only makessense if the Earth were a sphere. If the Earth were flat, it would sometimes cast a thinshadow, but it never does. Pretty clever, those ancient Greeks.

One final note. Because of tides from the Earth ,the Moon is slowly moving away from the Earth, by about4 centimeters a year.

As it recedes, it's slowly getting smaller in the sky. This means that, eventually, itwill be too far away to completely cover the Sun, and we won't get any more total eclipses.

Doing the rough math, that will be in about a billion years. Better watch eclipses while you can.

CHAPTER SEVEN

TELESCOPES

Space Telescope

I've talked a lot about observing the night sky with your eyes; just simply going outand seeing what you can see. It's pretty amazing what you can learn just by doing that,and of course that's all we humans could do for thousands of years.

But now we can do better. We can use telescopes.

The first person to invent the telescope is lost to history; despite"common knowledge,"

Galileo did not invent them. He wasn't even the first person to point one at the sky,or the first person to publish results! But he was a loud and persistent voice over theyears, and his amazing string of discoveries using his crude instrument landed him firmly in the history books. Aggressive self-marketing sometimes pays off.

You might think the purpose of a telescope is to magnify small objects so we can seethem better.

That's how a lot of telescopes are marketed, but to be honest that's notexactly the case. If you want to be really general, the purpose of a telescope is tomake things easier to see: To make the invisible visible, and to make the things already visiblevisible more clearly.

A telescope works by gathering light. Think of it like a bucket in the rain: The biggerthe bucket, the more rain you collect. If your bucket is big enough, you'll get plentyof water even when it's only sprinkling out.

In the case of a telescope, the "bucket" is an optical device like a lens or a mirrorthat collects light. We call this device the objective, and the bigger the objective, themore light it collects. Look at your eyes... well, that's tough, so let's think aboutour eyes for a moment. They also work as light buckets, but they only collect light through our pupils, which even under the best of circumstances are less than a centimeter across;a very tiny bucket indeed.

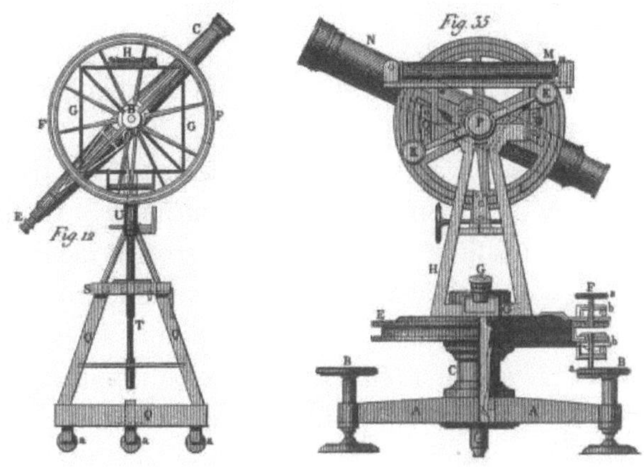

Ancient Telescopes

But we can do better. To extend the analogy, a telescope is like a bucket with a funnelat the bottom. All that light that it collects is then concentrated, focused, and sent intoyour eye. It turns a trickle of light into a torrent.

The amount of light it collects depends on the area of the objective. That means if youdouble the diameter of the collector, you'd collect four times as much light, becausethe area of the collector goes up as the square of the radius. Make a bucket 10 times wider,and you collect 100 times as much light! Clearly, as telescopes get bigger their ability toshow us faint objects increasesenormously.

In fact that was one of Galileo's first and most important discoveries: Stars thatwere invisible to the naked eye were easily seen through his telescope, even though itonly had a lens a few centimeters across. Those faint stars didn't emit enough light for his eyes to see them, but when he increased his collecting area with a telescope,they popped into visibility.

The primary way telescopes work is to change the direction light from an object is traveling.

I can see a star with my eye because light from that star is sent in my direction, intomy eye. But most of that light misses my eye, falling to the ground all around me.

The telescopecollects that light, bounces it around, and then channels it into my eye.

When the very first telescopes were built, this changing of the direction of light wasdone using lenses. When light goes from one medium to another – say, from going throughair to going through water or glass – it changes direction slightly. You see this all the time; a spoon sitting in a glass of water looks bent or broken. The spoon is doing justfine, but the light you see from it is getting bent, distorting the image. This bending iscalled refraction.

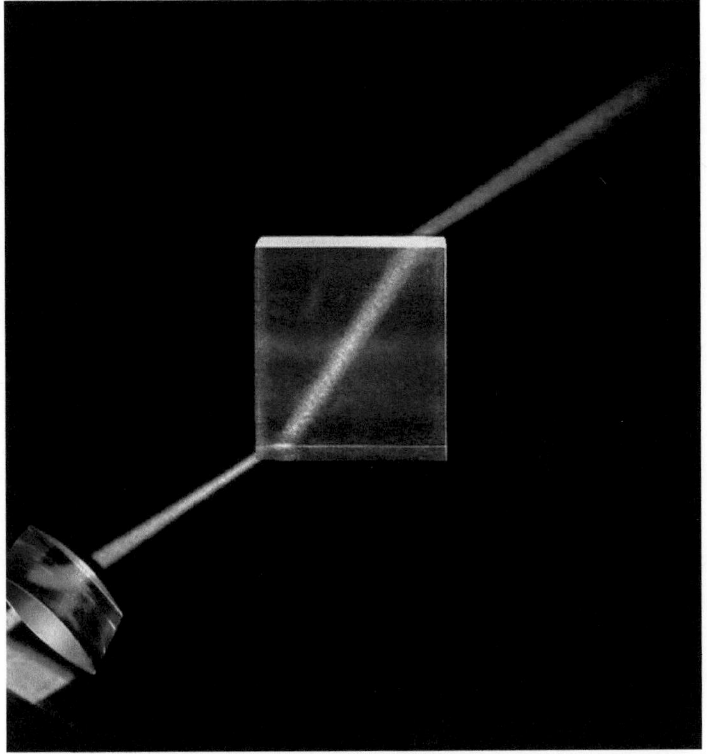

Refraction of Light

The way light bends depends on what's bending it (like water or glass) and the shape ofthe object doing the bending. It so happens that if you grind a piece of glass into alens shape, it bends -- or refracts -- the incoming light in a cone, focusing it intoa single spot. It's a light funnel!

This refraction has a couple of interesting results. For one thing, the light from thetop of a distant object is bent down, and the light from the bottom is bent up. When this light comes to a focus, it means you see the object upside-down! It also flipsleft and right, which can be a little disconcerting, and takes getting used to when you're usinga refracting telescope.

For another thing, the lens can magnify the image. That's again because the light isbent, and the image created of object observed can appear larger than the object does byeye. It depends on a lot of factors including the shape of the lens, the distance to theobject, and how far away the lens is, but in the end what you get is an image that looks bigger.That has obvious advantages; a planet like Jupiter is too far away to see as anythingother than a dot to the eye, but a telescope makes it appear bigger, and details can thenbe seen.

When Galileo and other early astronomers pointed their telescopes at the sky, multitudes were revealed: Craters on the Moon, the phases of Venus, Jupiter's moons, the rings ofSaturn, and so much more. The Universe itself came into focus.

When astronomers talk about using a telescope to make details more clear, they use a termcalled resolution. This is the ability to separate two objects that are very close together.

You're familiar with this; when you're driving on a road at night a distant car comingtoward you appears as a single light. When it gets closer, the light separates out—resolves— into two headlights.

A telescope increases resolution, making it easier to, say, split two stars that are closetogether, or to see details on the Moon's surface.

The resolution depends in part on the size of the objective; in general the bigger the telescope objective the better your resolution is.

Resolution is more useful than magnification when talking telescopes. Fundamentally, there is a limit to how well your telescope resolves two objects, but there's no limit to howmuch you can magnify the image. If you magnify the image beyond what the telescope can actuallyresolve, you just get mush.

Refracting telescopes are great, but they suffer from a big problem:

Big lenses arehard to make. They get thin near the edge, and break easily. Also, different colors oflight bend by different amounts as they pass through the lens, so you might focus a redstar, say, and a blue one will still look fuzzy.

No less a mind than Isaac Newton figured a way around this: Use mirrors. Mirrors alsochange the direction light travels, and if you used a curved mirror you can also bringlight rays to a focus. Telescopes that use mirrors are called reflectors.

The advantages of reflectors are huge: You only have to polish one side of a mirror,where a lens has two sides. Also a mirror can be supported along its back, so they canbe manufactured much larger more easily and for less money.

Although there have been many improvements made over the centuries, most big modern telescopes at their heart are based on the Newtonian design, and in fact no large professional-grade telescopes made today havea lens as their objective. Nowadays, it's all done with mirrors.

There's a third aspect to telescopes that's very important, beyond resolution and makingfaint things easier to see. They can literally show us objects outside of the range of colorsour eyes can see.

Ancient Telescopes

In the year 1800, William Herschel discovered infrared light, a kind of light invisible to our eyes. In the time since we've learned of other forms of invisible light:

radio,microwave, ultraviolet, X-rays, and gamma rays. Astronomical objects can be observedin all these flavors of light, if we have telescopes that are designed to detect theseflavors of light. Radio waves pass right around "normal" telescopes, ones that we useto observe visible light. X-rays and gamma rays pass right through them as if they aren't even there.

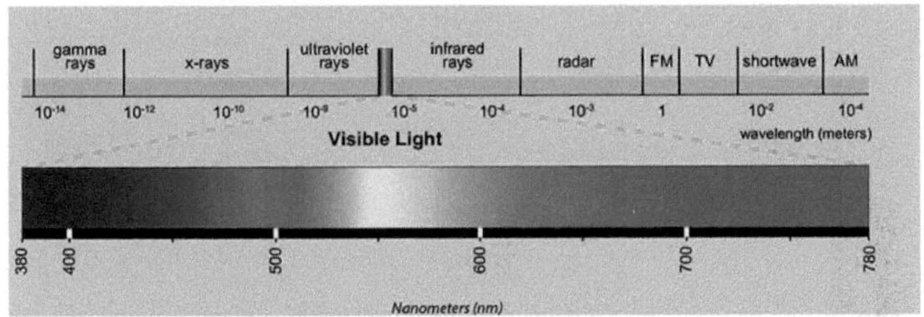

Electromagnetic Spectrum

But we're smart, we humans. We learned that giant metal dishes can and will bend radiowaves, and can be formed just like gigantic Newtonian mirrored telescopes. In fact, differentforms of light need different kinds of telescopes, and once we figured out how, we've built them.. We can now detect cosmic phenomena across the entire spectrum of light, fromradio waves to gamma rays, and have even built unconventional telescopes that detect subatomicparticles from space as well, such as neutrinos and cosmic rays. Because of this, we havelearned far more about the Universe than Galileo could have imagined.

Ancient Telescopes

And we're in the midst of another revolution, too. The actual biophysics is complicated,but in a sense our eyes act like movie cameras, taking pictures at a frame rate of about 14images per second. That's a short amount of time. Photographs, though, can take farlonger exposures, allowing the light to build up, allowing us to see much fainter objects.

The first photographs taken through a telescope were done in the 1800s. This has led to innumerablediscoveries; for example, in the 20th century giant telescopes with giant cameras revealeddetails in distant galaxies that led to our understanding that the Universe is expanding.

And now we have digital detectors, similar to the ones in your phone camera, but farlarger and far more sensitive. They can be dozens of times more light-sensitive than film, ableto detect in minutes objects that would've taken hours or more to see using film. These digital cameras can also be designed to detect ultraviolet light, infrared, and more. Wecan store vast amounts of that data easily on computers, and use those computers to analyzethat huge ocean of information, performing tasks too tedious for humans.

Most asteroidsand comets are discovered using autonomous software, for example, looking for movingobjects among the tens or hundreds of thousands of fixed stars in digital images.

This has also ushered in the era of remote astronomy; a telescope can be on a distant mountainand programmed to scan the sky automatically. It also means we can loft telescopes intospace, above the sea of air in our atmosphere that blurs and distorts distant, faint objects.

Space Telescopes

We can visit other worlds and send the pictures and data back home, or put observatories likethe Hubble Space Telescope into orbit around the Earth and have it peer into the vast depths of the Universe.

I would argue that the past century has seen a revolution in astronomy every bit as important as the invention of the telescope in the first place. In the early 17th century the entiresky was new, and everywhere you pointed a telescope there was some treasure to behold.

But with our huge telescopes and incredibly sensitive digital eyes now, that's still true.

We learn more about the Universe every day, just as we learn that there's more to learnevery day, too. That's one of the best parts of being an astronomer; the Universe is likea jigsaw puzzle with an infinite number of pieces. The fun never ends.

And remember: Even with all the wonders revealed by telescopes, your eyes are still prettygood instruments, too. You don't need big fancy equipment to see the sky. The importantthing is to go outside. Look up! That's fun too.

CHAPTER EIGHT

THE GRAVITY OF THE SITUATION

Astronaut in zero gravity

We live on a planet.

I mean, sure. But this isn't the natural state of the Universe; or, at least, it'snot the way things usually are. Most of the Universe is pretty empty — that's whywe call it "space" — and if I were to magically transport you someplace randomlyin the cosmos, the chances are you'd be a million light years from the nearest substantial object.

Evolving on a planet has warped our sense of physics. If I throw an object away fromme, it comes back. That's bizarre! It should just keep going, moving away from me at aconstant speed. Instead though it goes up, slows, stops, then falls back down toward me.

The difference between living on a planet and being in deep space is gravity. Gravityfrom an object goes on forever, but it gets weaker rapidly with distance. A zillion light years away, the Earth's gravity is fantastically weak, but here on Earth it's literally a force to bereckoned with. And in some places it can be a lot stronger than what we experience right here.

For most of history, gravity was just a fact of life, neither understood nor examined terribly closely. In the mid 1600s, scientists like Robert Hooke and Isaac Newton started investigating it using math — in fact, the two men got into a bitter feud over who thought of whatfirst. But whoever it was who first got it right, now we have a much better understanding of how gravity works.

One thing before we get to gravity. An important concept that comes up a lot is mass. It'sa bit tricky to define, but you can think of it as how much stuff makes up an object.

I know, that's not very scientific sounding, but it's not a bad way to think about it.

Something with more mass has more stuff in it.

Size doesn't really play into this; two objects can have the same mass but one canbe much larger than the other. In that case, the bigger object's mass is more spreadout, so we say it has lower density, where density is how much mass is inside a given volume.

In science terms, mass tells us how much an object resists having its motion changed.

An object with more mass is harder to get moving than an object with less mass, whichis pretty obvious if you've ever tried pushing on a toy car versus a real truck. But massis also defined using gravity.

Everything that has mass also has gravity and can inflict this force on another object.

The amount of force you feel from the gravity of an object like a planet depends on threethings: How much mass it has, how much mass you have, and how far away you are from it.

In fact, distance dominates here; the force of gravity weakens with the square of thedistance. Double your distance from an object and the force of gravity drops by 2 x 2 = 4times. Go 10 times farther away and the force drops by 10 x 10 = 100 times.

Gravity is also attractive: It can only draw things in, not repel them.

But how it attractsthings is where it gets fun.

If I hold up a rock and let go of it, it falls to the ground. What might be hard to see isthat it gets faster the longer it drops. Forces accelerate objects, so the longer the forceacts, the more the object's velocity changes – in this case getting faster. If I dropa rock from higher up, it'll move faster when it hits the ground. Other forces acton moving objects, as well, like friction and air resistance, counteracting gravity,making this acceleration hard to see. But in space, the force of gravity becomes very clear.

Two objects that have mass will attract each other. If there are no other forces actingon them, they'll accelerate toward each other until they meet. Remember, though, thatthe force of gravity depends on those masses. If one is really massive, and the other notso much, then in more practical terms the massive one will pull in the less massiveone. The more massive one does move, but much less than the other one.

When objects are free to move under the effects of gravity, we say they are in orbit. Thesimplest kind of orbit may not be what you think: It's actually just a line! When you drop a rock, it's very briefly in orbit. Ignoring things like the Earth's rotation(which adds a bit of sideways motion) it's close enough to say the rock just falls straight down, and is stopped because the Earth itself gets in the way.

That's not a terribly interesting orbit! So what if, instead of dropping the rock,we throw it? That gives it a little bit of sideways motion, so instead of hitting the ground at my feet, it hits a bit farther away. If I throw it harder, it moves horizontallyeven more before it hits.

What if I throw it really hard?

This is where Newton's genius comes in. He realized that if you throw the ball hardenough sideways, it will fall at the exact same rate the Earth would curve away underneathit. As Douglas Adams said in "Hitchhiker's Guide to the Galaxy," flying is just falling and missing the ground. It turns out, that's exactly what orbiting is, too.

A rock thrown hard enough sideways will fall toward the Earth, but always miss it, goinginstead into a circular path around it, guided only by gravity. It will orbit the Earth ina circle, taking about 90 minutes to go around the planet once.

Circles are simple orbits. The speed at which the orbiting satellite travels depends onthe mass of the object it's orbiting, and its distance from it. The farther it is, theweaker gravity is, so it doesn't have to travel as quickly to maintain the orbit.

Roughly 400 years ago, the astronomer Johannes Kepler realised that there can be other shapesof orbits as well. He discovered the planets orbit the Sun on ellipses, when previouslyit was thought they orbited in perfect circles. An elliptical orbit happens when you throwthe rock sideways even harder than it takes for a circular orbit; it goes up higher on one end of the orbit than on the other.

In fact, the harder you throw the rock, the more elongated the orbit gets. An orbit likethis is still closed; that is, the orbit repeats itself and the rock is still bound to theEarth by gravity. At some point, though if you throw the rock hard enough, an amazing thing happens: It can escape.

orbit is now a hyperbola, which is similar to a parabola, but is evenmore open. The rock never stops, even at infinity. It just keeps movin' on.

Like all forces, gravity gets weaker with distance. But its force never quite dropsto zero; it just gets smaller and smaller as you get farther and farther away.

So why then are astronauts on the space station "weightless"?

Gravity is still pulling on the astronauts! In fact, at the height of the station, Earth'sgravity has only decreased by a little bit; it's still about 90% as strong as it ison the Earth's surface. If they were in a tower 320 kilometers high they'd weigh90% of what they do on the Earth's surface. But the big difference is that the astronauts are in orbit, falling around the Earth. Weight is actually not just the force of gravityon a mass, but how hard a surface pushes back on that mass. For example, when you standon the ground, the ground pushes back. Otherwise you'd fall through! The force of the groundback on you is what causes you to have weight.

Weightlessness

In free fall, there's nothing pushing back. You're falling freely, and so you have noweight. NASA likes to call this condition "microgravity," since there are subtleforces acting on you.

This actually highlights the difference between mass and weight. In space you have the samemass as you do on Earth, but no weight. If another astronaut pushed on you they'd haveto exert a force, but if you stood on a scale in space it wouldn't register anything.

Space is weird. Well, compared to Earth.

One more thing, and this is truly weird: Photons, particles of light, have no mass, yet theycan be affected by gravity, too, bending their direction of flight as they pass a massiveobject! It turns out gravity can actually warp space! Light travels along the fabricof space like a truck on the road, and if the road curves, so does the truck.

CHAPTER NINE

OUR SOLAR SYSTEM

The Solar System

The Solar System is the name we give to our local cosmic backyard.

A better way to thinkof it is all the stuff held sway by the Sun's gravity: The Sun itself, planets, moons, asteroids,comets, dust, and very thin gas.

If you took a step back — well, a few trillion steps back — and looked at it from the outside,you might define the solar system as: the Sun. That's because the Sun comprises morethan 98% of the mass of the entire solar system.

The next most massive object, Jupiter, isonly $1/10^{th}$ the diameter and less than 1% the mass of the Sun.

But that's a little unfair. Our solar system is a pretty amazing place, and you can figureout a lot of what's going on in it just by looking at it.

Planets orbitting around the sun

For thousands of years we had to explore the solar system stuck on this spinning,revolving ball — the Earth. The problem was, for a long time we didn't know it wasa spinning, revolving ball. Well, the ancient Greeks knew it was a ball — they had evenmeasured its size to a fair degree of accuracy — but most thought it was motionless.

When a few folks pointed out that this might not be the case — like the ancient Greek astronomerAristarchus of Samos — they got ignored. The idea that the sky spins around the Earthseems obvious when you look up, and when great minds like those of the astronomer Ptolemyand philosopher Aristotle supported that idea, well, people like Aristarchus got left behind.

The basic thinking was that the Moon, Sun, and stars were affixed to crystal spheresthat spun around the Earth at different rates. While it kinda sorta worked to predict themotions of objects in the sky, in detail it was really unwieldy, and failed to accurately predict how the planets should move.

Still, Ptolemy's idea of a geocentric Universe stuck around for well over a thousand years.

It was the year 1543 when Nicolaus Copernicus finally published his work proposing a Sun-centeredmodel, much like the one Aristarchus had dreamed up 2000 years previously.

Unfortunately, Copernicus'smodel was also pretty top-heavy, and had a hard time predicting planetary motions.

The last nail in geocentrism's coffin came a few years later, when astronomer JohannesKepler made a brilliant mental leap: Based on observations by his mentor Tycho Brahe,Kepler realized the planets moved around the Sun in ellipses, not circles as Copernicus had assumed. This fixed everything, including those aggravating planetary motions. It stilltook a while, but heliocentrism won the day. And the night, too.

This paved the way for Newton to apply physics and his newly-created math of calculus todetermine how gravity worked, which in turn led to our modern understanding of

around the solarsystem, but most are in the main belt.

Then, out beyond the orbit of Neptune is a collection of rocky ice balls, called KuiperBelt Objects. The biggest are over a thousand miles across, but most are far smaller. Theytend to follow the plane of the planets too. But if you go even farther out, starting tens of billions of kilometers from the Sun, that disk of Kuiper Belt Objects merges into avast spherical cloud of these ice balls called the Oort Cloud. They don't follow the planeof the inner solar system, but orbit every which way.

So what do all these facts tell us about the solar system? We think they're showing ushints of how the solar system formed.

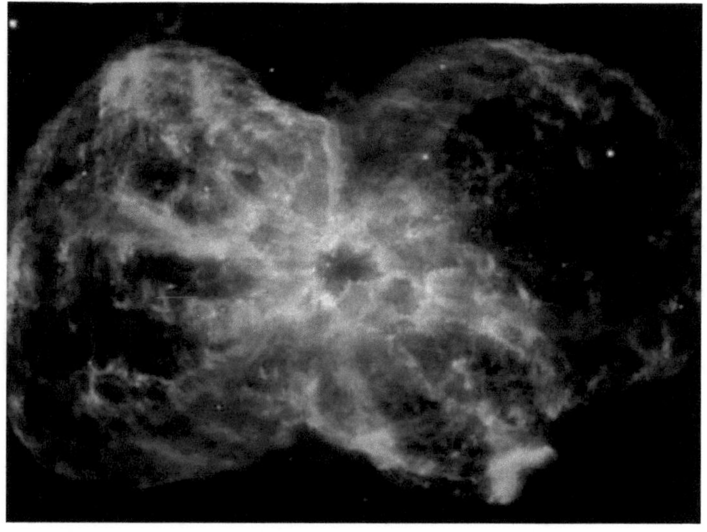

The gaseous cloud

4.6 billion years or so ago, a cloud floated in space. It was in balance: its gravity tryingto collapse it was counteracted by the merger internal heat that buoyed it up. But thensomething happened: Perhaps the shockwave from a nearby exploding star slammed intoit, or maybe another cloud lumbered by and rammed it.

Either way, the cloud got compressed, upsetting the balance, and gravity took over. It started to collapse. As it did, angular momentum became important. That's a lot like regular momentum,when an object in motion tends to stay in motion. But in this case it's a momentumof spin, which depends on the object's size and how rapidly it's rotating. Decreasethe size, and the rotation rate goes up. The usual analogy is an ice skater starting aspin, then drawing their arms in. Their spin is amplified hugely.

The same thing happened in the cloud. Any small amount of spin it had got ramped upas it collapsed. It flattened into a disk, much like spinning raw pizza dough in the air will flatten it out.

As it collapsed, material fell to the centre, getting very dense and hot. Farther out inthe disk, where it was cooler, material started to clump together as little grains of dustand other matter randomly bumped into other little bits. As these clumps grew, their gravity increased, and eventually started drawing more material in. These little blobs are called planetesimals — wee baby planets.

As they grew, so did the center of the disk. The object forming there was a protostar — or,spoiler alert, the protosun. Eventually its center got so hot that hydrogen fused into helium, with makes a lot of energy.

A lot of energy.

A star was born. The new Sun blasted out fierce light and heat that, over millions of years, blew away the leftover disk material that hadn't yet been assimilated into planets.

The solar system was born.

Closer to the Sun it was warmer. Hydrogen and helium are very light gases, and the warmbaby planets there couldn't hold on to them. Farther out, there was more material in thedisk, and the planets were bigger. Since it was cooler, too, they could hold on to thoselighter gases, and their atmospheres grew tremendously, eventually outmassing the solidmaterial in their cores. They became gas giants.

Enter Caption

There was also a lot of water out there, far from the Sun, in the form of ice. Smallericy objects formed past Neptune, but space was too big and random encounters too rare.

They didn't get very big, maybe a few hundred kilometers across. A lot of them — billions, perhaps trillions of them — got too close to the big planets, and were flung hither and yon.

Closer in, material between Mars and Jupiter couldn't get its act together to form aplanet either; Jupiter's gravity kept agitating it, and impacts between two bodies tendedto break them up, not aggregate them together.

And there you have it. Our solar system, formed from a disk, sculpted by gravity. Echoes ofthat disk live on today, seen in the flatness of the solar system.

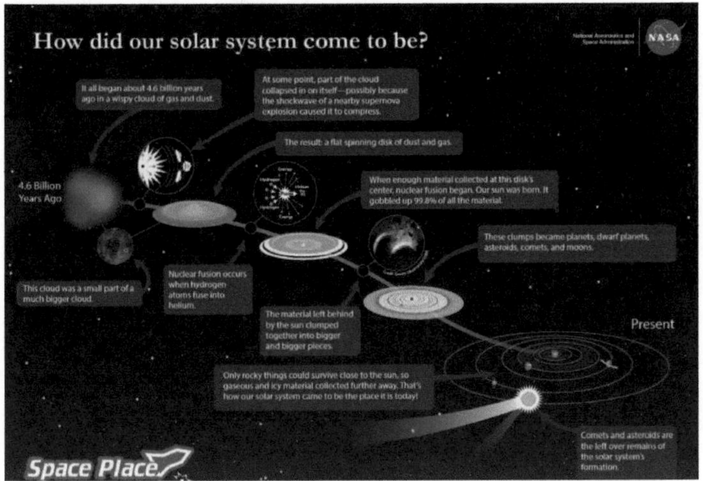

Formation Of Solar System

This isn't guesswork: the math and physics bear this out. And not only that, we see ithappening, now, today. When we look at gas clouds in space, we see stars forming, we see protoplanetary disks around them, we see the planets themselves getting their start.

We may think of ourselves as the solar system, but we're really just a solar system. Thescenario that happened here so long ago plays itself out daily in the galaxy. We're oneof billions of such systems.

And remember: Every atom in your body, and everything you see around you — every tree, every cloud, every human, every computer, everything on Earth, even the Earth itself— was once part of that dense cloud.

We are, quite literally, star stuff.

CHAPTER TEN

THE SUN

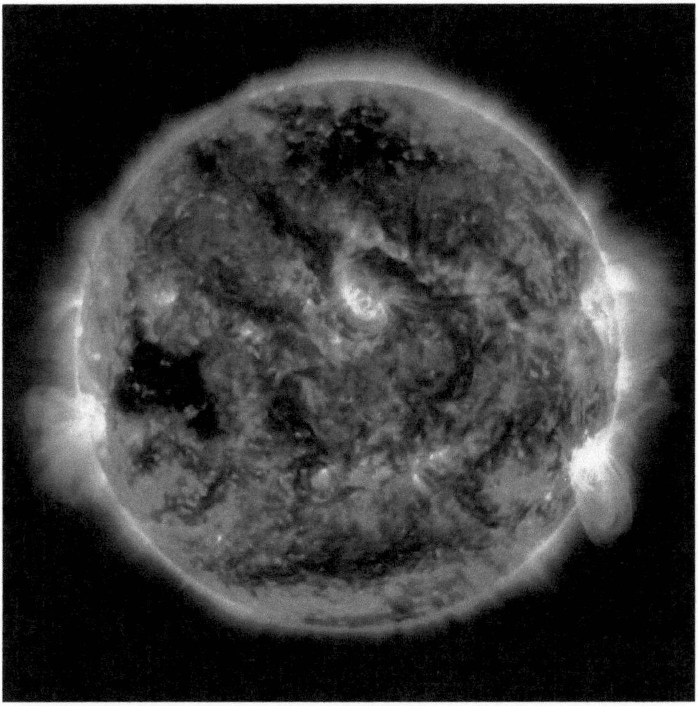

The Sun

The sun is a star.

That's a profound statement, and one that's not really all that obvious.

Those littlesparks in the night sky are pretty, but don't look anything at all like the hot, blazingorb that lights up our days. It was a pretty remarkable intellectual leap to understandthe Sun and the stars are just different flavors of the same kind of object. The only differenceis that the Sun is close, but the stars are terribly far away, so they're fainter.

Right away, let's clear up a misconception: A lot of people say the Sun is a middle-sized,average star. But that's not fair. Sure, it's somewhere in the middle of the sizerange of stars, but the vast majority of stars are dim red dwarfs, far smaller than the Sun.

By size and number, the Sun ranks in the top 10% of stars in the galaxy! In our solar system,it's clearly the dominant object: brighter, more massive, and more influential than anything else.

But, what is it?

The Sun is, essentially, a big hot ball of mostly hydrogen gas. It's 1.4 million kilometersacross — more than 100 times the Earth's diameter, and big enough that well over amillion Earths could fit inside of it. And it's massive: 300,000 times more massivethan the Earth, a staggering two octillion tons of gas.

But if we want to truly understand the Sun, we have to look into its heart.

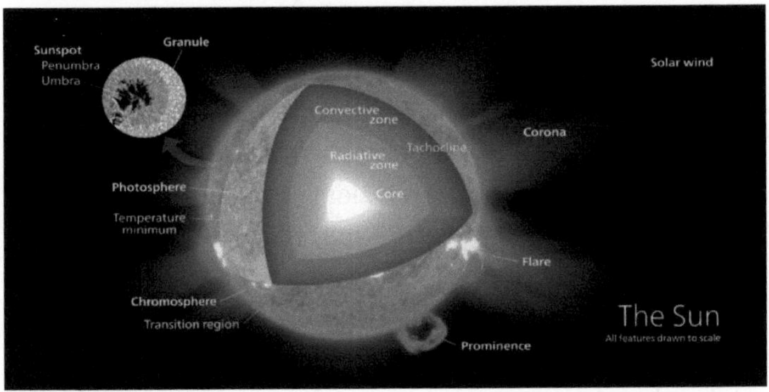

Features of Sun

At the very core of the Sun, conditions are hellish. The pressure is a crushing 260 billion times the Earth's atmospheric pressure, and it's a searing 15 million degrees Celsius.

Under those conditions, hydrogen is completely ionized, which means the electrons in theatoms are stripped from their protons. This makes the core a thick soup of ultra-hot subatomicparticles. In fact, the protons are squeezed together so hard by the octillions of tonsof mass lying on top of them that an amazing thing happens:

They fuse together.

Through a complicated series of steps, the hydrogen atoms fuse together to form the heavierelement helium. Along the way, some of the nuclear energy stored in those atoms is released.

That amount of energy is described by Einstein's famous equation E=mc2, which states that masscan be converted into energy, and vice-versa.

Atoms are pretty small, though, so each helium atom made in the Sun's core generates onlya tiny bit of energy... but a lot of helium atoms are made. A lot. Get this:Every second of every day, the Sun converts 700 million tons of hydrogen into 695 milliontons of helium. The missing 5 million tons — the equivalent weight of 15 Empire StateBuildings — is converted into energy, and that's a lot of energy.

Enough, in fact, to power a star.

It's equivalent to detonating 400 billion one megaton nuclear bombs every single second.

That's millions of times the entire nuclear arsenal of our planet. Every second.

And that's why, even from a distance of 150 million kilometers, the Sun is so brightyou can't even look at it. Even from that distance, its heat can be felt on your skinwhen you stand outside.

Hydrogen fusion occurs in the core of the Sun. The energy released heats the gas abovethe core, but not quite enough to fuse hydrogen into helium. Further from the Sun's centerthe gas becomes less dense, and at some point the heat pouring up from below makes the gasbuoyant: it rises, in the same way a hot air balloon on Earth rises. This process is calledconvection, and it's an efficient way of transferring heat. Huge columns of risinghot gas stretch hundreds of thousands of kilometers high, bringing the Sun's internal heat tothe surface. The gas then cools and sinks back down into the interior. We can actuallysee the tops of these columns, packed together across the Sun's face.

Above the convecting layer is a much thinner, cooler layer very near the Sun's surfacecalled the photosphere, or literally the sphere of light. This is where the density of thematerial inside the Sun gets thin enough that it becomes transparent; light can shine right through it. At this point, the energy from inside the Sun is free to travel into space.

It's this light that we see when we look at the Sun.

The Sun is a gas and doesn't have a solid surface, but the gas in the photosphere thinsrapidly compared to the Sun's huge size that you can think of it as the Sun's surface.

And there's one final layer above that: The ethereally thin corona, sort of like theSun's atmosphere. It's less than 1% as dense as the photosphere, but actually much hotter; temperatures there can reach over a million degrees! However, it's so thinlydispersed that it's incredibly faint, and can only be seen during a total eclipse, orusing special telescopes that block the intense light from the Sun itself. The corona extends for millions of kilometers.

And in a sense it doesn't actually end. The corona merges into what's called the solarwind, a stream of subatomic particles moving away from the Sun. It blows out in all directions,though mostly along the Sun's equator. The speed of the wind is usually about a millionkilometers per hour — yes, seriously — and can reach speeds even much higher even than that.

When hydrogen fuses into helium in the Sun's core, the energy is released in the form oflight. This light immediately smacks into a subatomic particle, which absorbs it, convertsa little bit of the energy into motion, and re-emits the light with a little bit lessenergy. The light works its way out of the Sun this way, losing energy every time itencounters a particle, until eventually it gets to the surface, and is free to fly awayinto the Universe as a much lower-energy photon of visible light.

So how long does this process take?

I've seen different numbers for it, some as much as a million years. But a lot of thosecalculations don't model conditions inside the Sun accurately; for example they don'ttake into account the gas convecting for hundreds of thousands of kilometers. More modern calculationsshow that it takes closer to 1 or 200,000 years for the energy to work its way out.

That's still a pretty long time: The light you see from the Sun now got its start inthe Sun's core around the time Homo sapiens first appeared in Africa!

The Sun's surface is, to put it kindly, a mess. And the key to that mess is magnetism.

I've been saying the Sun is made of gas, but that's not entirely accurate. It'sso hot inside the Sun that electrons are stripped from their parent atoms in the gas, creatingwhat's called a plasma, a gaseous soup of charged particles. These moving electric chargegenerates a magnetic field.

The interior of the Sun is essentially all charged particles in motion. Convection, coupledwith the Sun's rotation, sets up rivers or streams of plasma inside the Sun, eachgenerating and carrying its own magnetic field. When this plasma reaches the Sun's surface, their magnetic fields do too.

Maybe you've seen those looping arcs of magnetism around a bar magnet when it affectsiron filings on a piece of paper. The solar magnetic fields are like that, except therecan be zillions of them all over the Sun's surface, where they can interact and even get tangled up.

When the plasma reaches the surface, it cools. But if the magnetic loops tangle up, theyprevent the plasma from sinking back down into the Sun, like a knot in a shoelace preventsit from going through the eyelet on your shoe. Plasma shines because it's hot, but as itcools it dims. It sits on the surface, dimming, producing a dark spot on the surface of theSun, which we call... a sunspot.

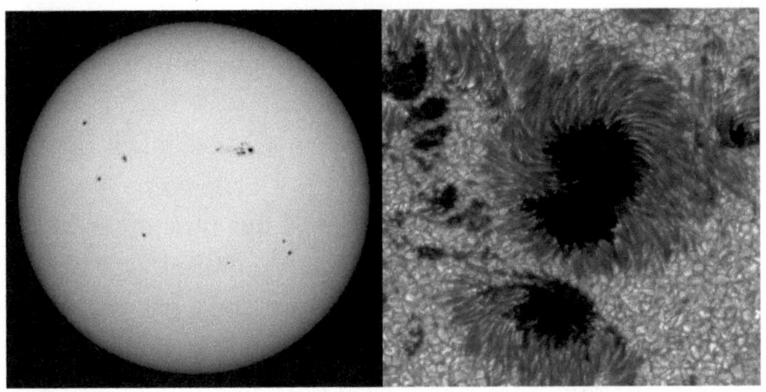

Sunspots

Sunspots can be huge; they commonly dwarf the entire Earth, and some are so big theycan be seen without using a telescope (as long as you're wearing adequate eye protection, of course).

Around the edges of sunspots, the magnetic field lines are concentrated. This can energizethe plasma even further, heating it up. This creates a bright rim around sunspots calledfaculae (Latin for "little torch"). The dark parts of sunspots dim the overall lightfrom the Sun, but faculae can be so intense they compensate forthat, and even add morelight.

Ironically, sunspots actually increase the energy output of the Sun.

Plasma on the Sun's surface can flow along these magnetic loops, too. This can createhuge arcs of material called prominences or filaments, stretching for hundreds of thousandsof kilometers across the Sun, looking like fiery arches.

We think these magnetic field lines are feeding energy from the Sun's surface into the corona,which is why it's so much hotter. It's not exactly clear how this happens, but scientistsare following several leads right now. This long-standing mystery may soon be solved.

Magnetic fields on the Sun also have a huge amount of energy stored in them. You can thinkof them like very tightly wound and very stiff springs. But remember, these magnetic fieldlines get tangled up. If conditions are right, they can actually snap, in essence creatinga gigantic short circuit. When this happens, all that vast energy stored in the lines explodes outwards all at once in an event we call a solar flare.

Even an average solar flare is mind-crushingly powerful; a big one can release as much as10% of the entire Sun energy output. This explosion blasts out high-energy light andlaunches material off the surface of the Sun at high speeds, sending it into interplanetary space.

Another type of solar eruption is called a coronal mass ejection, or CME. It's similarto a flare, but if a flare is like a tornado — intense and localized — a CME is likea hurricane, huge and strong. Like flares, they form when tangled magnetic field lineserupt, blasting out energy, but they occur higher off the Sun's surface.

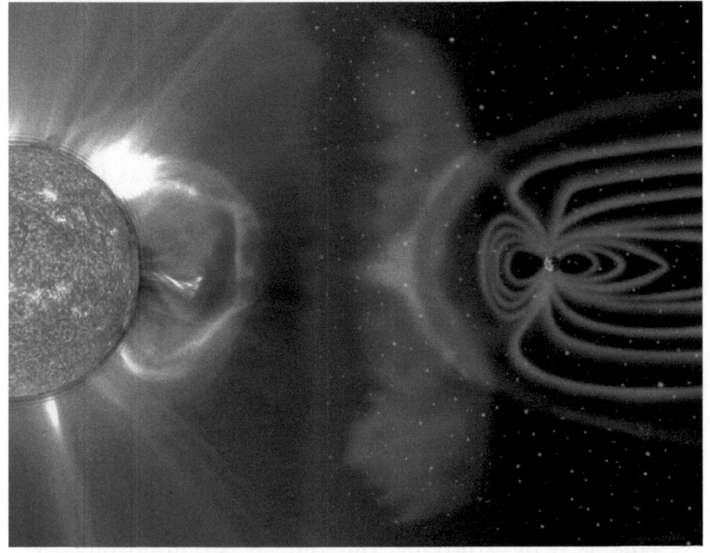

CME

Both flares and CMEs eject material into space — billions of tons of it, in fact. Thisblast of debris can hit the Earth, and when it does, there can be profound effects. Ouratmosphere absorbs the high-energy light, protecting us. Also, the subatomic particles are generally deflected by the Earth's magnetic field, so we're OK.

But, if conditions are right, the Earth's magnetic field can interact with the particles.

Massive numbers are funneled down into Earth's atmosphere near the poles, causing the airto glow. This is what we call the aurora, or the northern (and southern) lights. Dependingon the shape of the magnetic field, the auroras can form spectacular multicolored ribbons and sheets.

Not all the effects are benign, though. As the magnetic fields interact, they can inducevery strong currents of electricity in the Earth's crust. This can overload power grids,causing blackouts; in 1989 Quebec suffered a massive power outage from a solar storm.

The very first such storm ever detected was in 1859, and it was also the most powerfulever seen. If an event like that were to happen today, it could cause worldwide blackoutsand potentially be very damaging. Satellite electronics would be fried, too, and we dependon those satellites for our modern civilization. In fact, in 2012, a huge storm probably the equal of the 1859 event blasted away from the Sun... in another direction, missing theEarth. Had it hit us, well, you probably wouldn't be reading this now. We'd still be recovering.

This is why studying the Sun is so important. We depend on it for light and heat and thevery basis of life itself, but it's entirely capable of knocking our society to its knees.

Understanding it is critical to our future.

The Sun is the 2 octillion ton gorilla in the room. We need to respect that.

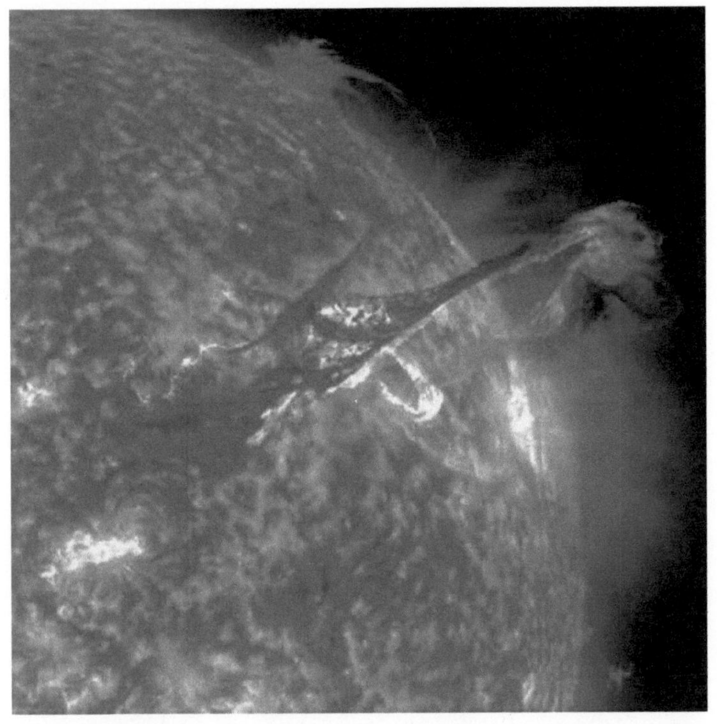

Closeup of The Sun

CHAPTER ELEVEN

THE EARTH

The Earth

The Earth is a planet.

That's a profound statement, and one that's not really all that obvious. For thousandsof years, planets were just bright lights in the sky, one-dimensional points that wandered among the fixed stars. How could the Earth be one of them?

With the invention of the telescope those dots became worlds, and with spacecraft they becameplaces. The Earth went from being our unique home in the Universe to one of many such...well, planets.

The Earth is the largest of the terrestrial planets, the four smaller, denser, rocky worldsorbiting close in to the Sun. It's about 13,000 kilometers across, and has a single, large Moon which we'll learn a lot more about next week.

Unlike the other three terrestrial planets, Earth has something very important: Water.Or, more specifically, liquid water on its surface, where it can flow around, evaporate,become clouds, rain down, and then mix up chemicals so they can do interesting, complex things—like support life.

Earth's ability to sustain life depends on that water. It also depends on Earth'satmosphere, of course—breathing has its advantages—and both, weirdly enough, dependon Earth's magnetic field to exist. And that, in turn, depends on what's going on deep inside our planet. So, let's take a look.

Like the Sun, the Earth is a many-layered thing. At its very center is the core, which actually has two layers, the inner core and the outer core.

The inner core is solid, and made mostly of iron and nickel. These are heavy elements,and sank to the center of the planet when it was forming, leaving lighter elements likeoxygen, silicon, and nitrogen to rise to the surface. The solid inner core is about 1200 kilometers in radius, or about 10% the radius of the Earth.

Inside The Earth

The outer core is also mostly iron and nickel, but it's liquid. The material in it canflow. It's about 2200 kilometers thick.

The temperature in the Earth's core is tremendously high, reaching 5500°C. The pressure is huge as well, as you might expect with the weight of an entire planet sitting on top of it.

You might think at such a high temperature, iron would be a liquid, but iron can staysolid if the pressure is high enough. In the inner core, the pressure is extremely high, and even though it's hot, iron is solid. In the outer core, where it's still hot,but the pressure is a little bit lower, iron is a liquid.

Above the core is the mantle.It's about 2900 kilometers thick. The consistency ofthe mantle is weird; most people think it's like lava, but really it's like very thickhot plastic. It behaves more or less like a solid, but over long periods of time, geologicperiods of time, it can flow.

On top of the mantle is the crust, a solid layer of rock. The overall density of therock in the crust is less than in the mantle, so in a sense it floats on the mantle. There are two types of crust on Earth: Oceanic crust, which is about 5 kilometers thick, and continental crust, which is a much beefier 30-50 kilometers thick. Still, the crust is very thin compared to the other layers.

The crust isn't a solid piece, though; it's broken up into huge plates, and these canmove. What drives the movement of these plates is the flow of the rock in the mantle, and that, in turn, is powered by heat.

The core of the Earth heats the bottom of the mantle. This causes convection; the warmer material rises. It's not exactly a speed demon, though: The rate of flow is only a couple of centimeters per year, so it takes about 50 or 60 thousand years for a blob to move a single kilometer.

The hot material rises toward the surface, but it's blocked by the crust. The magmaticrock pushes on the plates, causing them to slide around very slowly. Your fingernailsgrow at about the same rate the continents move. Over millions of years, though, thisadds up, changing the surface geography of the Earth—where you see continents now isnot at all where they were millions of years ago.

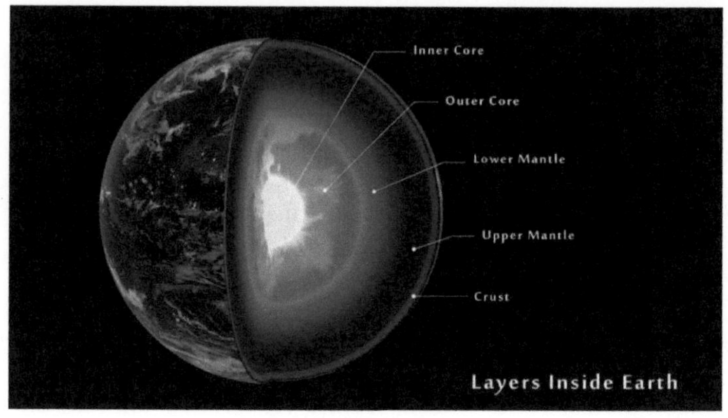

Layers of Earth

In some places, generally where the plates come together, the crust is weaker. Magma can pushits way through, erupting onto the surface, forming volcanoes. Other volcanoes, like Hawaiior the Canary Islands, are thought to be from a plume of hotter material punching its wayright through the middle of a continental plate. As the plate moves, the hot spot formsa linear chain of volcanoes over millions of years.

Volcanoes create new land as material wells out, but they also pump gas out of the Earth too. A large part of Earth's atmosphere was supplied from volcanoes!

The interior of the Earth is hot; in the core, it's about as hot as the surface of the Sun! Where did that heat come from?

Most of it is leftover from the Earth's formation, more than 4.5 billion years ago.

As rock and other junk accumulated to form the proto-Earth, their collisions heated them up. As the Earth grew that heat built up, and it's still toasty inside even today.

Also, as the Earth formed and gained mass it began to contract under its own gravity,and this squeezing added heat to the material.

Another source is elements like uranium deep inside the Earth, which add heat as the atomsradioactively decay. And a fourth source of heat is from dense material like iron and nickel sinking to the center of the Earth, which warms things up due to friction.

All of these things add up to a lot of heat, which is why, after all these billions ofyears, the Earth still has a fiery heart.

The outer core of the Earth is liquid metal, which conducts electricity. The liquid convects,and this motion generates magnetic fields, similar to the way plasma in the Sun generates magnetic fields.

The Earth's rotation helps organize this motion into huge cylindrical rolls that align with the Earth's axis. The overall effect generates a magnetic fieldsimilar to a bar magnet, with a magnetic north pole and south pole, which lie close to the physical spin axis poles of the Earth.

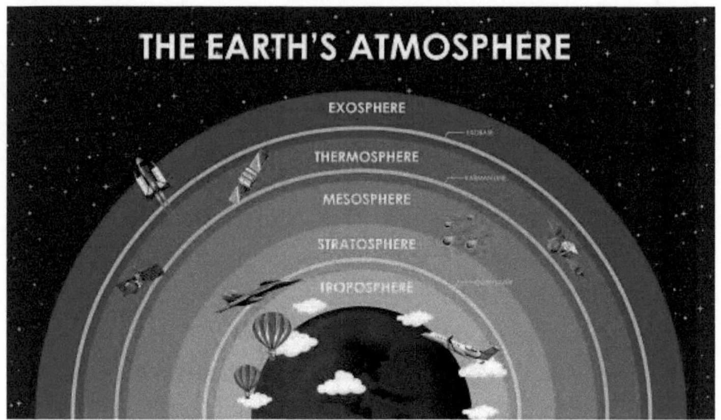

The Atmosphere

The loops of magnetism surround the Earth, and play a very important role: They deflectmost of the charged particles from the solar wind, and they trap some, too. Without thegeomagnetic field, that solar wind would hit the Earth's atmosphere directly. Over billionsof years, that would erode the Earth's air away, like a sand blaster stripping paintoff a wall. Mars, for example, doesn't have a strong magnetic field, and we think that'swhy its atmosphere is mostly gone today.

But we do have an atmosphere, and it's more than just air blowing around. Earth's atmosphereis the layer of gas above the crust. Because it's not solid, it doesn't just stop,it just sort of fades away with height. By accepted definition—theline between Earth's atmosphere and space is set at 100 kilometers up. This is what'scalled the Kármán line, and if you get above it, congratulations! You're an astronaut.

Aurora Borealis

The atmosphere is, by volume, about 78% nitrogen, 21% oxygen, 1% argon of all things, and then an assortment of trace gases. There's water vapor, too, almost all of it below a heightof about 8-15 kilometers. This part of the atmosphere is warmest at the bottom, whichmeans we get convection in the air, creating currents of rising air, which carry waterwith them, forming clouds, which in turn is why we have weather.

At a height of about 25 kilometers on average is a layer of ozone, a molecule of oxygenthat's good at absorbing solar ultraviolet light. That kind of light can break apart biological molecules, so the ozone layer is critical for our protection.

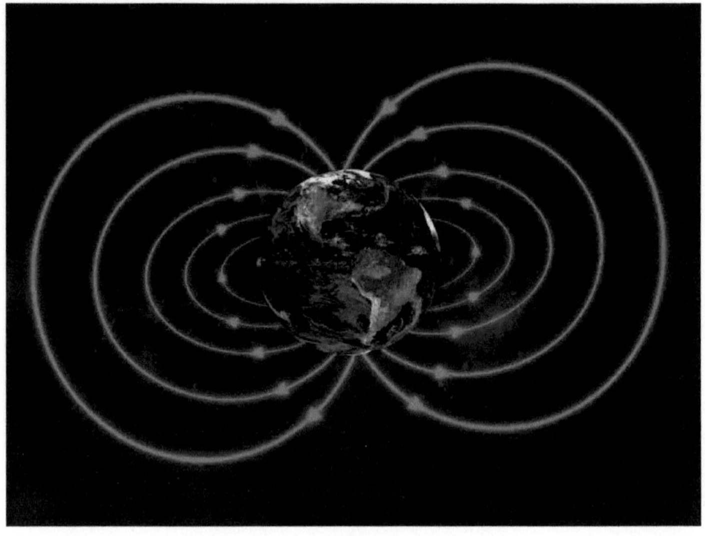

Earth's Magnetic Field

Incidentally, the Earth's magnetic field does more than trap solar wind particles;it also channels some of them down into the atmosphere, where they slam into air moleculesabout 150 kilometers up. This energizes the molecules, which respond by emitting light in different colors: Nitrogen glows red and blue, oxygen red and green. We call this glowthe aurora, and it happens near the geomagnetic poles—far north and south. The lights canform amazing ribbons and sheets, depending on the shape of the magnetic field.

You may not be aware of the atmosphere unless the wind is blowing, but it's there. Itexerts a pressure on the surface of the Earth of about a kilogram per square centimeter,or nearly ten tons per cubic meter! There's roughly ton of air pushing down on you rightnow! You don't feel it because it's actually pushing in all directions—down, to the sides, even up—and our bodies have an internal pressure that balances that out.

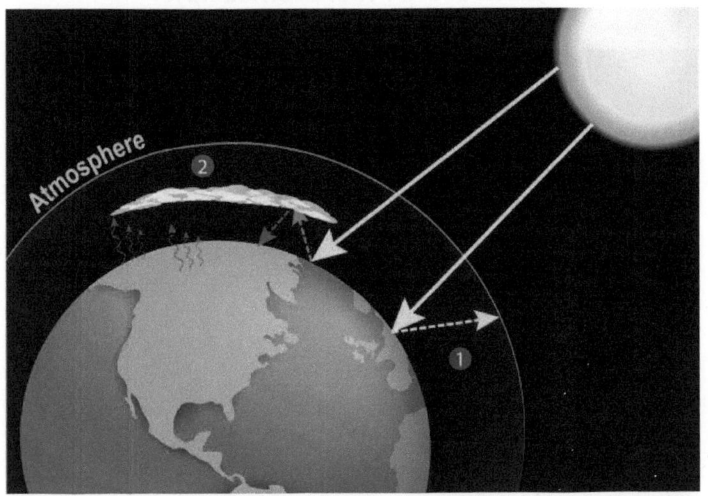

Earth's Atmosphere

The Earth also has liquid water on its surface, unique among the planets. The continentalcrust is higher than oceanic crust, so water flows down to fill those huge basins. TheEarth's surface is about 70% covered in water. Most likely, some of this water formed when the Earth itself formed, and some may have come from comet and asteroid impactsbillions of years ago. The exact proportion of locally sourced versus extraterrestrialwater is still a topic of argument among scientists.

Earlier, I mentioned trace molecules of gas in the atmosphere. One of these is carbondioxide, which only constitutes about 0.04% of the lower atmosphere. But it's critical.

Sunlight heats the ground, which emits infrared light. If this infrared light were allowedto radiate into space, the Earth would cool. But carbon dioxide traps that kind of light,and the Earth doesn't cool as efficiently.

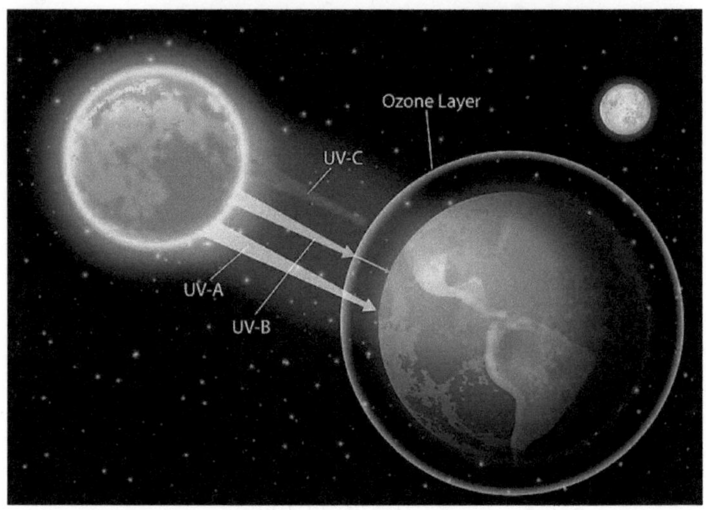

The Ozone Layer

This so-called greenhouse effect warms the Earth. Without it, the average temperatureon Earth would be below the freezing point of water! We'd be an iceball.

This is why climate scientists are concerned about carbon dioxide. A little is a good thing,but too much can be very dangerous. Since the Industrial Revolution, we've added alot of the gas to our atmosphere, trapping more heat. By every measure available, the heat content of the Earth is increasing, upsetting the balance. It's melting glaciers in Antarctica and Greenland, as well as sea ice at the north pole. Sea levels are going up, and some ofthe extra Carbon dioxide in the air is absorbed by the oceans, acidifiying them.

There's an old concept in science fiction called terraforming: Going to uninhabitable alienplanet and engineering it to be more Earthlike. I don't know what the opposite process wouldbe called, but it's what we're doing to Earth right now.

The Earth is the only habitable planet in the solar system. And you know what?

We should keep it that way.

Atmosphere From Space

CHAPTER TWELVE

THE MOON

The Moon

The Moon is pretty hard to miss when it's up at night. It's big and bright and reallyvery pretty. Even cooler, it's the closest astronomical object in theUniverse to us,and arguably, the one we know best.

I hate to break it to you, but we humans are pretty egotistical. Even though there areover 160 known moons of decent size in our solar system, we call ours THE Moon, witha capital M, like it's the only one, or the most important one.

And I guess to us it is the most important one. It's only the fifth largest moon inthe solar system in absolute size, but compared to Earth it's pretty big; fully a quarter of the diameter of the planet.

That's a way bigger ratio than for any other moon orbitinga major planet in the solar system.

By the numbers, the Moon is about 3470 kilometers in diameter, and on average about 380,000kilometers from Earth. That means it looks pretty big in our sky, but probably not asbig as you think.

When the moon rises, it can look huge and looming on the horizon, like you could fallinto it. Ah, but that's not really the case; it's easy to show it's the same size onthe horizon as it is high overhead. Yet people think it looks twice as big when it's onthe horizon! This is the well-known Moon Illusion, and it's due to two factors: how we perceivethe sizes of objects, and how we perceive the sky.

We don't really see the sky as a hemisphere over our heads, but more like a flattenedbowl, with the horizon farther away than the zenith. So when the Moon's on the horizon,our brains are convinced it's farther away. But if it's farther away, it must be physicallybigger to appear that size, right? So our brain interprets the Moon's size as HUGE.

It's an illusion, but a convincing one.

In fact, the Moon is about the same size as a small pill held up at arm's length! Oursatellite is a lot smaller than you think.

The internal structure of the Moon is roughly similar to the Earth: It has a solid, ironinner core; a liquid outer core, a thick mantle, and a crust of lighter material on top. The core is small, probably 350 kilometers in radius, and still hot, though not as hot asEarth's core. The lower mantle may be a thick fluid, but unlike Earth's mantle the upper part is solid.

The easiest part of the moon to observe is its surface, so of course we know the mostabout that. The near side, the side we see from Earth, is divided into two distinct typesof regions: highlands, which are heavily cratered, and maria—Latin for "seas"—which are darker and smoother.

The craters in the highlands are from countless impacts over the eons from asteroids and comets.

Rocks from these regions have been dated to be well over 4 billion years old — nearlyas old as the Moon itself!

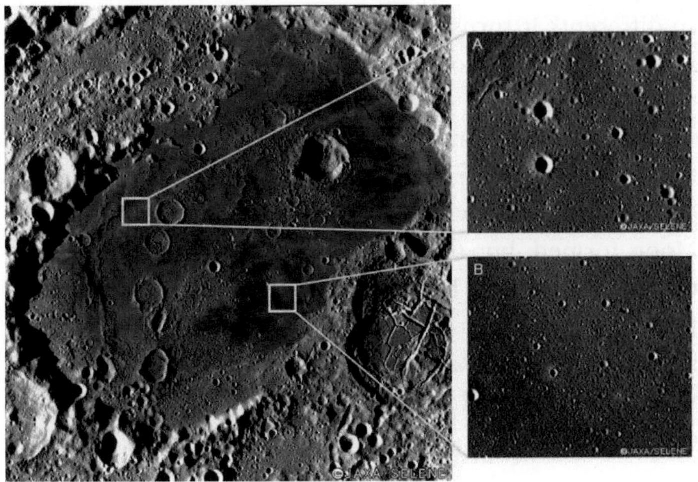

Craters on Moon

The maria, on the other hand, don't have nearly as many craters. They're younger,but that's relative; rocks from those areas appear to be roughly 3-3.5 billion years oldon average. The maria are made of darker, basaltic material, which means they probablyformed from lava flooding older areas.

For most of human history, the far side of the Moon was hidden from us, but in 1959 theSoviet Union flew the Luna 3 space probe around the Moon, photographing the far side for thefirst time. Everyone expected it to look a lot like the near side, but shockingly, it'svastly different: There were almost no maria! That's weird; the near side is covered withthem. And not only that, observations from subsequent lunar probes showed the crust onthe lunar far side is thicker than it is on the near side as well.

The Moon is starting to stack up mysteries. Why is it so big compared to Earth? Why arethe near and far sides so different? It turns out the composition of the crust has a lotof similarities to Earth, but also a lot of differences as well. Why?

It turns out the answers to these questions are all related to how the Moon formed 4.5 billion years ago.

A lot of ideas have been proposed to figure out how the Moon formed, but the best onegoing these days is called the Giant Impact hypothesis. When the solar system formed,there were a lot more objects orbiting the Sun than there are now. These ranged in sizefrom grains of dust up to objects the size of planets, and that meant there were lots of collisions.

No doubt the Earth suffered many such impacts. But one happened late in Earth's history,relatively speaking, roughly 50 million years after things started to settle down.

A Mars-sizedplanet, given the unofficial name Theia, slammed into our young planet, but it wasn't a head-onimpact; it was a grazing collision.

The impact was colossal, blasting a huge amount of material from both planets into space.

Most of it came from the outer layers of the Earth, since the collision was a grazing one.

This material rapidly coalesced into the Moon, and that explains why there's some but nottotal similarity in composition to Earth; it used to be part of the Earth. But someof it came from the other planet, too. And we may even have some evidence of it; somerocks from the Moon show a peculiar ratio of different kinds of oxygen atoms, calledisotopes. It's possible some of the more exotic isotopes of oxygen came from the other planet.

Actually, this idea has been around for a long time, ever since the Apollo missions in the 1970s. There's a lot of evidence to support it, too. But a new twist on it goes farther.

When the Moon formed from the debris of the collision, it was close to Earth, probably20,000 kilometers away. The collision was so violent that it completely melted the Earth,and the Moon was molten too. Tidal forces rapidly synchronized the Moon's spin and orbital period, so that one face always pointed toward Earth. If you were on that side ofthe Moon, the Earth would dominate the sky, appearing 80 times larger than the Moon appears in our sky today.

And the Earth was hot. It hung there like blast furnace, and would've seriously heatedthe near side of the Moon.

The far side would've been much cooler. The material on the nearside would've vaporized, and a lot of it would have condensed on the far side.

South Side of Moon

Overtime, this created the thicker far side crust we see today.

Then there was another seriously terrifying event: the Late Heavy Bombardment, a periodof intense collisions with comets from the outer solar system, probably triggered bythe movement of outer planets. This rain of millions of comets left scars on all the inner worlds, including the Moon. That's when most of the highland cratering occurred.

Some of these collisions were massive, carving gigantic craters on the Moon. Later, lavabubbled up through cracks in the Moon's surface, flooding these craters, creating the maria we see today.

Ah, but the far side's crust was thicker. Impacts there couldn't get as deep, and itwas harder for lava to break through and bubble up. That explains why there are so few maria there.

This idea that the Earth cooked the Moon and formed the crustal anomaly is pretty new,and is still being argued over. There are also competing hypotheses about this, as well.

As we gather more evidence, we'll eventually get a better understanding of just why theMoon's crust is so weird.

After all that, I have to say: it's a little unfair to divide the lunar surface today intojust highlands and maria. For example, craters are pretty diverse. Some are small and simplebowl shapes. Others are huge, dozens of kilometers across and more, punctuated with a centralpeak, a mountain in the middle that formed as material from the gigantic impact thatformed it splashed back up in the middle. Double craters are common too, probably formed when binary asteroids hit the Moon. There are also crater chains: long lines of smallcraters that may have formed when a nearby large impact splashed out long streamers of material.

Rays are common from big craters, too. These are extremely long "splash marks" pointingradially out from the impacts, probably formed when plumes of material were ejected. Someof the brightest are from the crater Tycho in the Moon's southern hemisphere, and theystretch for 1500 kilometers. The material is a bit more reflective than the surroundingterrain, so they appear bright in contrast, and are one of the most outstanding features visible near the time of the full Moon.

And there's so much more! Long, sinuous rilles like dry river beds wind their wayacross the surface, actually the sites of ancient lava flows. There are lava tubes aswell, where the top of a lava flow cooled and formed a tunnel through which lava couldflow for long distances. Sometimes the roof, as it's called, collapses and forms a skylight,and we can see into the otherwise hidden tunnel.

There are also cliffs, mounds, ancient and quite dead volcanoes, even mountain chains!

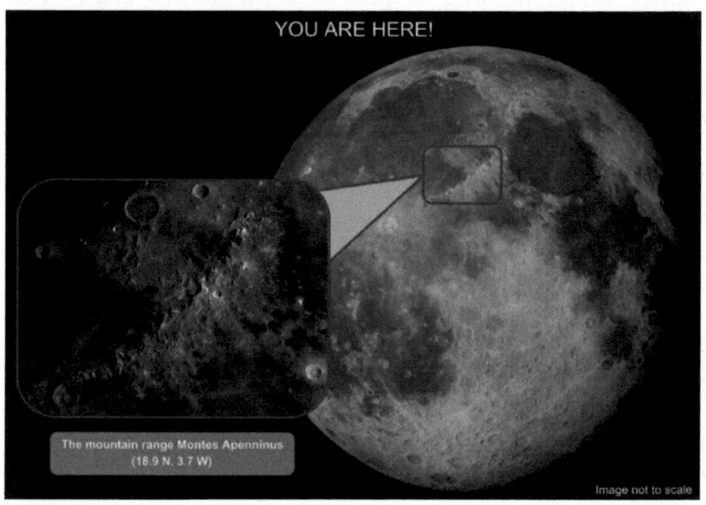

Mountain Ranges On Moon

There's no tectonic activity on the Moon, but mountain ranges formed at the edges ofgiant impacts, where the huge forces unleashed pushed up the rocks at the crater rim.

And new observations show there's something else on the Moon, too: Water. Deep craters

near the Moon's poles have floors that never see sunlight. Comet impacts can distributewater all over the

Moon, but most of it is destroyed by sunlight. But it can collectin these dark craters, and studies show there could be over a billion tons of water therein the form of ice. That would be a huge boon to colonisation; water is heavy and reallyexpensive to transport from Earth. If it's already on the Moon, that makes it a lot easier to put people there.

And that's in our future, I have no doubt. We're starting to get serious about going back to the Moon; NASA has plans of returning, and other countries like China and India arelooking Moonward as well. It's not a matter of if, but when. And it could be soon – sosoon that, I'd bet, there's a really good chance the next person to step foot on theMoon is already alive. Perhaps some teenage student in some country is just now takingan interest in science, math, engineering - an interest that will one day will lead to another giant leap for humanity.

Man On Moon

Man's Footprint On Moon

Man On Moon

American Flag On Surface Of Moon

CHAPTER THIRTEEN

THE MERCURY

The Mercury

Mercury is the closest planet to the Sun. As you might expect, that makes it pretty hot.

But also, it's pretty cool.

There are seven naked-eye solar system objects in the sky: Mercury, Venus, Mars, Jupiter,

Saturn, the Sun, and the Moon. Seven. Each of them was associated with a god in ancient times. Mercury was the Roman messenger of the gods, fleet of foot—literally, he hadwings on his shoes—and a rapid traveler.

To anyone who's seen Mercury in the sky, this affiliation with the swift god is nosurprise. Mercury the planet moves pretty quickly, visibly changing its position relativeto the background stars even after a single night.

Despite its speed, the planet never gets very far from the Sun. At best, it can reach aseparation of about 28°. That's about three times the apparent size of your fist held at arms length.

In 1639 the Italian astronomer Giovanni Zupi used a telescope to observe Mercury, and hediscovered it undergoes a complete cycle of phases over time, just like the Moon does.

The only way that can happen is if Mercury orbits the Sun, and not the Earth — another checkmark in thecolumn for heliocentrism, which was starting to look better and better all the time.

And of course that's the way things really are. Mercury is the innermost of the planetsin the solar system. It orbits the Sun at an average distance of about 58 million kilometers,roughly a third the distance of the Earth from the Sun. That's why we never see itstray far from the Sun. From our viewpoint, its smaller orbit keeps it huddled closer to our star.

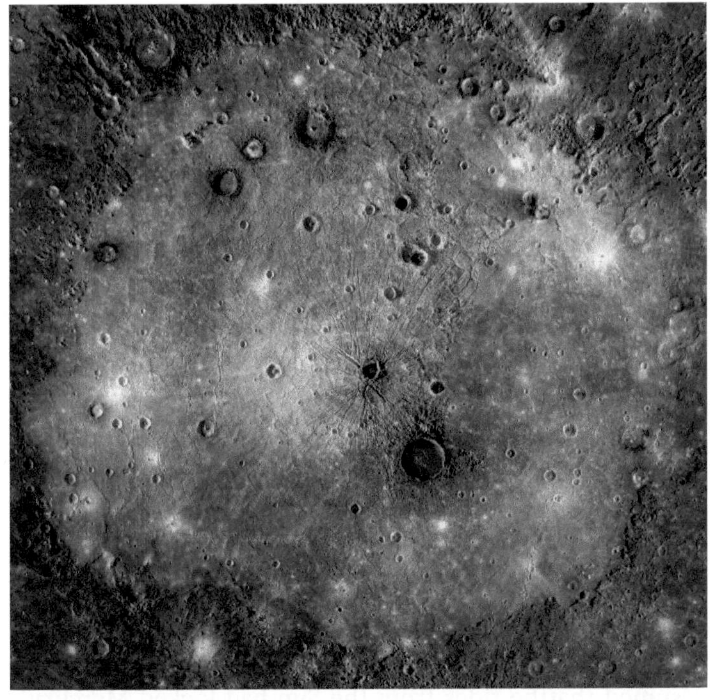

The Mercury

That's why we see it move so rapidly, too; it's closer to the Sun, so the gravity itfeels from the Sun is stronger, and therefore its orbital velocity is faster than Earth's.

It orbits the Sun once every 88 days.And that's also why we see undergo phases. When it's between us and the Sun we're looking at its dark side, and when it's on the other side of the Sun we're lookingat its fully illuminated half. In between it goes through the same phases as the Moon:crescent, half full, gibbous, and so on.

The largest is called Caloris Basin, a whopping huge impact feature 1600 kilometers across.

There are some smoother plains on the planet's surface too, which appear to be older thanthe cratered regions. These plains are covered in cracks called rupes. These are compressionfolds, like wrinkles on a fruit rind that's dried out. Apparently, as Mercury's interiorcooled after it formed, the planet shrank, and the crust cracked as it tried to shrink as well.

Several of the craters have extensive ray systems. Like on our Moon, these are formedwhen impacts fling out long plumes of material that then settle down on the surface.

Craters On Mercury

One of my favorite things of all about Mercury: Craters are named after artists. Musicians,writers, painters, and more, so we have craters like Botticelli, Chekov, Debussy, Degas, Okyo,Sibelius, Vivaldi, and Zola. There's even one named Tolkien!

Dipping below the surface, we can only infer what Mercury's internal structure is like.

But the planet's dense, nearly as dense as Earth. We know the surface is rocky, soto be as dense as it is it must have a large iron core, far larger in proportion to the planet than Earth's. Mercury's core may reach ¾ of the way to the planet's surface!

tobe abundant on the surface.

Speaking of which, here's a fun fact: pound for pound, impacts on Mercury are more violentthan they are on Earth. Mercury has weaker gravity, so it doesn't pull in impactorsas hard as the Earth does, but it orbits the Sun far faster than Earth does, so asteroidsand comets tend to hit at higher velocity. That makes the explosive energy higher, makingcraters bigger.

And there's one more surprise Mercury has, and it's really surprising: Despite beingso close to the Sun, and having a surface temperature that can reach 430°C — 800°Fahrenheit — astronomers have found water ice on Mercury!

It exists in the bottoms of deep craters near Mercury's poles, where sunlight never reaches.

These are called "cold traps," and temperatures there don't get above -170° C. It's notknown for sure where the water comes from, but it's likely to be from comets and asteroidsthat impacted the planet, scattering the water across the surface. Of course, in the harsh heat that water just goes away. But in those deep craters it can persist, accumulating over the eons. There may be billions of tons of it there!

It's bizarre to think that in one of the hottest places in the solar system there canbe conditions so cold ice can exist, but one thing we've learned about nature over andagain: It has a lot more imagination than we do.

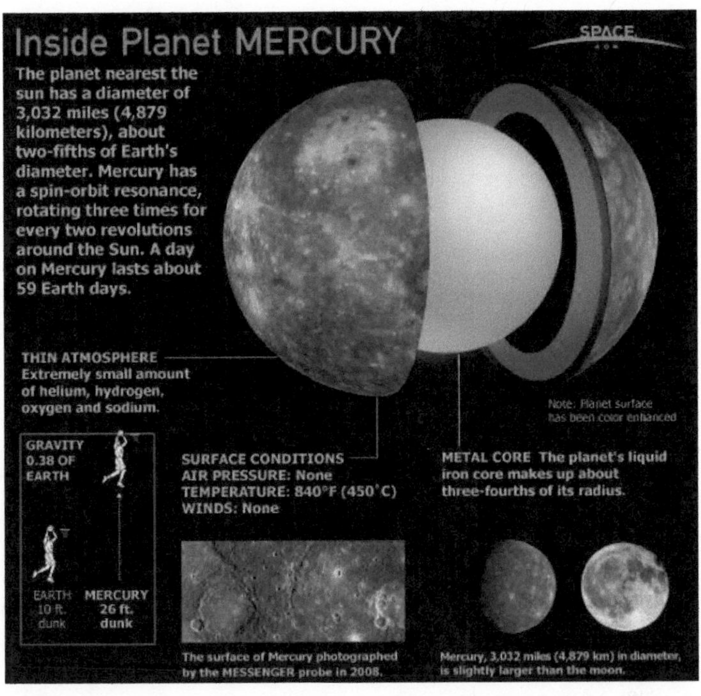
Inside Planet MERCURY
SPACE
The planet nearest the sun has a diameter of 3,032 miles (4,879 kilometers), about two-fifths of Earth's diameter. Mercury has a spin-orbit resonance, rotating three times for every two revolutions around the Sun. A day on Mercury lasts about 59 Earth days.
THIN ATMOSPHERE Extremely small amount of helium, hydrogen, oxygen and sodium.
Note: Planet surface has been color enhanced
GRAVITY 0.38 OF EARTH
EARTH 10 ft. dunk
MERCURY 26 ft. dunk
SURFACE CONDITIONS
AIR PRESSURE: None
TEMPERATURE: 840°F (450°C)
WINDS: None
METAL CORE The planet's liquid iron core makes up about three-fourths of its radius.
The surface of Mercury photographed by the MESSENGER probe in 2008.
Mercury, 3,032 miles (4,879 km) in diameter, is slightly larger than the moon.

CHAPTER FOURTEEN

THE VENUS

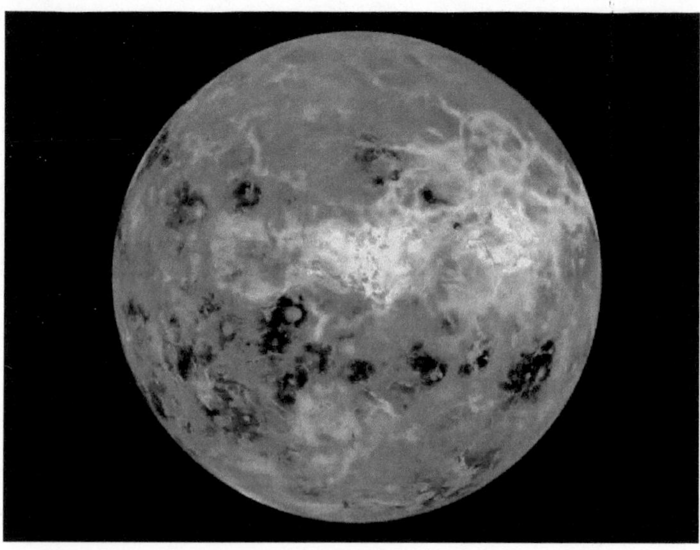

The Venus

Venus was the Roman goddess of love, and honestly, if you've ever seen it after sunset, hanginglike a diamond in the twilight, the planet Venus is stunningly beautiful.

The only problem? Venus is hell.

Venus is the second rock from the Sun, closer to the Sun than Earth is. It's the thirdbrightest natural object in the sky after the Sun and Moon, and it's shockingly bright when you see it, in fact, a lot of the time when people see it they think it's an airplane.

Some folks—and this is true—even report it as a UFO.

Like Mercury, it never gets far from the Sun; at best it can reach about 45° away. If youwant to see it, the best time to look is after sunset or before sunrise.

Through a telescope, Venus can be seen to undergo phases just like the Moon and Mercurydo, too. When it's on the far side of its orbit from Earth, we see the illuminated face,so it looks full. As it rounds the Sun and approaches Earth in its orbit, it gets biggerfrom our point of view, because it's getting closer, but it also wanes; it's gibbous,then half full, then a crescent.

When it gets between the Sun and Earth, it's as close as it can get to us, about 45 millionkilometers away. It's a very thin crescent at that point, but close enough to us thatyou can see the phase easily with just binoculars. Ironically, even though we see only a small portion of it illuminated then, it appears so big that it's actually brighter thanwhen it's full but far away.

The orbit of Venus around the Sun is tipped with respect to the Earth's by a littleover 3°. So, like the Moon as seen from Earth, Venus usually passes above or below the Sunin the sky as it laps the Earth and pulls ahead in its orbit.

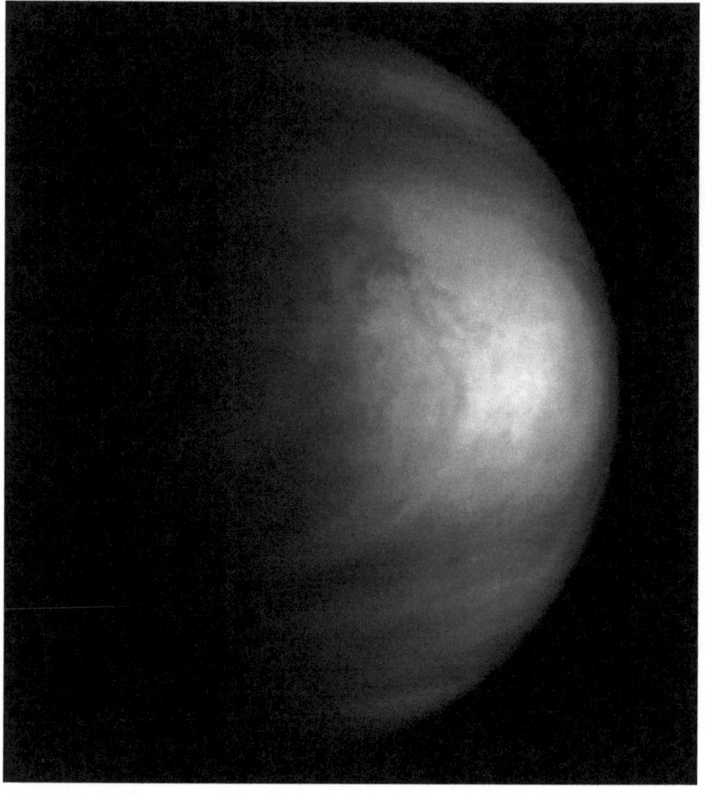

But again, just like with the Moon, sometimes things line up just right and Venus passesdirectly across the Sun's face. This event is called a transit. During a solar eclipse the Moon can completely block the Sun, but Venus is much farther away, so it can onlyblock about a tenth of a percent of the Sun. We see the planet as an inky black circleagainst the Sun's face.

Transits were very important centuries ago. Scientists realized that by precisely timingthe start and end of a Venus transit, and applying a little geometry, they could figureout how far away Venus was, and use that like a meter stick to measure the size of the entiresolar system. Grand expeditions were sent to remote parts of the Earth where the transitswere visible, but it turns out Earth's atmosphere blurs the disk of Venus just enough that exacttiming of the transit isn't possible.

Scientists had to wait until we could use radar and other methods to get the exact distancesto planets in the solar system, but transits are still pretty amazing to watch. They'revery rare: the way the orbits of Venus and Earth align, they happen in pairs separatedby eight years, but then don't happen again for over a century. The last pair of Venustransits happened in 2004 and 2012.. But the next one? December 10, 2117. If youmissed the last two, sorry about that.

Venus is actually so bright sometimes that it can be seen in broad daylight.. So here's an obvious question: Why is Venus so bright? Telescopic observationsshow it to be a nearly featureless white disk, completely covered in a thick cloud layer,reflecting almost all of the sunlight that falls on it. OK, great, so that's why it's bright, but then why are its clouds so thick?

Well, it turns out that Venus might be nice to look at from a distance, but up close,Not so nice.

In some ways, Venus is the planet in the solar system most similar to Earth. It's onlya wee bit smaller — 12,100 kilometers across, about 95% the width of the Earth — and has80% the Earth's mass. But if it's a twin of Earth, it's the evil twin.

Venus is closer to the Sun. At a distance of about 110 million kilometers, 2/3rds thedistance of the Earth from the Sun, you'd expect it to be warmer. What you might notexpect is that its surface temperature is 460° Celsius—that's 860° F, hot enough to melt lead.

And it gets worse. Its air is almost entirely composed of carbon dioxide, and atmosphericpressure on Venus is a crushing 90 times that of Earth's! As if that's not bad enough,it rains sulfuric acid, too, but it's so hot the drops evaporate before hitting the ground.

Yep. Venus is hell.

Why? How did it get so hot? It turns out Venus is a victim of a runaway greenhouse effect.

A long time ago, Venus may have been more temperate, and might have even had liquidwater oceans. But the Sun was cooler when it was younger, and as it aged it got hotter.

At some point, the thinking goes, the Sun warmed Venus enough that its oceans startedto evaporate. Water vapor is an excellent greenhouse gas, so Venus's heating accelerated.

It got so hot the oceans boiled away. Any carbon dioxide dissolved in the water wasreleased to the atmosphere, heating the planet even further, and thickening the atmospherehugely. It got so hot that the Carbon dioxide even got baked out of the rocks, which was like, well,throwing gasoline on a raging fire. The greenhouse effect raged out of control at that point.

Venus lacks a magnetic field, so it has no protection from the solar wind blasting pastit. Over billions of years, this stripped a lot of the lighter elements from the atmosphere,as well as all of the water. The resulting atmospheric chemistry is pretty screwy comparedto Earth. Sulfur dioxide is a popular molecule there, and clouds form from sulfuric acid.

Those clouds are high off of the surface, and very white and reflective.

It's pretty incredible to think about. The Sun warmed, so Venus warmed, and then a cascadingseries of events lead to it being a ridiculously hostile environment due to the runaway greenhouseeffect. Even though Mercury is closer to the Sun, Venus is way hotter!

Given that, the last thing you might expect on Venus is... snow. Well, possibly; observationsshow that there's something shiny on the mountaintops, and snow fits the bill. Butit's not water ice like on Earth. As the thinking goes, at lower elevations, mineralslike bismuthinite and galena would be vaporized by the heat. They'd then circulate up intothe atmosphere and deposit onto the surface at mountaintops where it's cooler. If thisis correct, then Venus is so bizarre it literally snows metal there!

There's other weird stuff going on at Venus, too. For one thing, it has an incredibly slowrotation rate: One day on Venus is about 243 Earth days! It rotates so slowly that at itsequator, you could jog faster than the planet spins. Its slow spin is probably why it hasno magnetic field, too, since rotation is critical in generating the magnetic fieldsof objects like the Earth and the Sun.

Not only that, but the planet spins backwards! This is called retrograde motion, and in asense it means Venus's north pole got swapped with its south pole: It flipped over.

It's not clear why that happened. A lot of ideas have been proposed, including a giantcollision that skidded the planet's spin to a halt, but as of right now, Venus'slazy rotation is still not completely understood.

If you could survive it, living on Venus would be really odd. The thick clouds mean it'sabout as bright as twilight on Earth, despite being closer to the Sun. The thick atmosphere alsomeans surface temperature is about the same everywhere on the planet, pole to equator.

Due to its backwards rotation, the Sun would rise in the west, and due to the slow rotationits day is actually longer than its year! Calendars on Venus would be a mess.

But calendars would probably be the least of your worries if you had to live there.

Incidentally, Venus has no moon. Being closer to the Sun, it's possible that any moonit may have once had would have been perturbed by the Sun's gravity, and was eventuallytossed out of Venus's grasp. It's also possible it simply never had one to begin with.

And here's another fun fact: Venus is the most spherical of all the planets. Becauseit rotates so slowly, it doesn't bulge out at the equator from centrifugal force like Earth does. The diameter from pole to pole is almost exactly the same as it is throughthe equator. We don't have a lot of data about the interiorof Venus, though given its similar composition and size to Earth, it's not too crazy tothink it has a core, mantle, and crust like we do. But even given the weird atmosphere,the surface of Venus is really different than ours.

Venus doesn't have tectonic activity like Earth does; it's thought that water helpsdrive that, and Venus long ago lost its water to the greenhouse effect. Still, the surfaceappears to be very young; about a thousand impact craters have been found, and they'reevenly distributed around the planet. The majority appear to be in pretty good shape,they haven't been eroded much, indicating they aren't terribly old. Not only that,but the erosion we do see seems to be about the same for all these craters, indicatingthey're all roughly the same age!

That's weird! This all points to some sort of catastrophic event that resurfaced theplanet roughly half a billion years ago. Any features older than that were wiped out, andthen big impacts over time created the craters we see now. But what could repave an entire planet?

A big clue can be found by counting volcanoes on Venus: There are 167 bigger than 100 kilometersin diameter, a huge number. These volcanoes could, over time, pump out enough lava tocover the entire surface of Venus. There's also a lot of indirect evidence that volcanicactivity is ongoing, now, today: One mountain on

Venus, called Idunn Mons, is seen to beabnormally warm, for example, indicating it might have magma under its peak. Also, sulfurdioxide levels dropped a lot in the 1980s, which may indicate a big volcanic event happenedin the 1970s, blasting out lots of the gas, which then subsided. It's possible, though somewhat speculative, that the entire planet is a supervolcano, a ginormous pressure cookerof barely-constrained magma. Every few hundred million years, the whole surface lets go ina colossal eruption, covering everything in lava.

Some volcanic features on Venus are different than on Earth. Without tectonics, slow bubbling leaks of lava from the interior of the planet can continue in one spot for a long time.

This creates what are called "pancake domes": huge, flat, low domes. Many are dozens ofkilometers across, but less than a kilometer high. The lava that formed them was probablyreally viscous, which is why the domes are flattened and spread out. The searing surfacetemperature of Venus probably kept the lava hot and helped it spread out more, too.

Oh, and one final note: under international agreement, surface features on Venus—mountains, plains, craters, and so on—are all named after women or goddesses of variouscultures. This is an homage to the planet itself being named after a goddess, of course.

Interior of Planet Venus

CHAPTER FIFTEEN

THE MARS

The Mars

You know, I can't think of any object in the sky that's captured our imagination like Mars has.

The Red Planetwas once thought to be the god of war, and in more modern times has been the setting

for a zillion science fiction novels, movies, TV shows, and more. And now that we've gonethere, landed there, roved there, it's become far more than a simple background for an alieninvasion story: It's become a world, a place... and maybe, one day, a destination.

Mars is the fourth planet from the Sun, and the outermost of the terrestrial planets;that is, ones that are rocky and similar in size to Earth. It orbits on average a little over 200 million kilometers from the Sun. That puts it outside Earth's orbit, andit never gets much closer to us than about 60 million kilometers. It's colder than us, too, with an average surface temperature of about 60 below 0 Celsius. It's not aterribly big planet; it's only about half the size of Earth. Still, when it's closestto us in space it shines brightly in our night sky, a red beacon glowering like an angry eye.

No doubt this is why ancient civilizations associated it with war! But it turns out Marsisn't red because it's bloody. It's red because it's rusty. Literally.

That red color you see comes from fine-grained dust on the surface, almost like ruddy talcumpowder. The dust is rich in iron that's oxidized, forming rust. The dust coats a lotof the surface, giving it a butterscotch or ochre coloring, and also gets blown into the atmosphere.

A lot of the surface of Mars is also grey volcanic rock called basalt, and togetherwith other minerals gives Mars its overall reddish look.

We can get a decent view of Mars from Earth using telescopes, but small features are maddeningly difficult to tease out.

The idea of a clement environment on Mars stuck with us, though... at least until the1960s and 70s, when we started send probes to the planet. They did not see a lovely,habitable world: Instead, what we got were photos of a dry, dead, forbidding planet.

The surface geography of Mars is weird. There's a huge dichotomy between the northern hemisphere, which is mostly smooth plains, and the southern, which is cratered, hilly highlands. Apparently,Mars suffered a tremendous impact from an object hundreds of kilometers across eonsago. It left behind a vast basin near the north pole of the planet, which filled with lava. Topographic maps show the northern hemisphere has much lower elevations than the southern, and can be depressed by several kilometers. Walking from the south to the north pole isessentially all downhill!

Another large feature is the Tharsis bulge, a huge plateau that's home to the four biggestvolcanoes on Mars, and the largest volcanoe in the solar system: Olympus Mons. Mars doesn'thave plate tectonics today, but there's evidence it once did. Tharsis was probablyover a hot spot, a plume of hotter material rising up through the planet's mantle. That'swhat may have created the bulge, and as the plate slowly moved the plume punched throughthe crust to create the chain of three smaller (but still huge) volcanoes.

Surface Of Mars

But the grandest of the surface features on Mars is easily Valles Marineris; a canyondiscovered when the Mariner 9 probe orbited Mars in the 1970s. It's a gigantic crackin the surface of Mars 4000 kilometers long, 200 kilometers wide, and 7 kilometers deep.

That's 10 times longer and 10 times wider than the Grand Canyon! Unlike the Grand Canyon, it wasn't carved by water; it may have formed when the Tharsis bulge rose up, creating thevalley as a radial crack in the surface.

Mars, like Earth, has polar ice caps. Both are mostly water ice, several kilometers thick,but they get seasonal coatings of dry ice, frozen carbon dioxide, that covers them from1 to 8 meters thick. This happens in their respective winters; in the summer, sunlightthaws the CO2, turning it directly into a gas which then blows away from the pole, generating fierce winds.

Speaking of which, Mars has an atmosphere, but it's thin. Pressure at the surface isless than 1% of Earth's, and the air is mostly carbon dioxide. In fact, as much as a third of the Martian atmosphere freezes out every winter to coat the polar ice caps!

The air doesn't provide much of a shield from asteroid and comet impacts, so the surfaceis heavily cratered—and it still gets hit today. The space probe Mars ReconnaissanceOrbiter has been circling Mars so long, it's actually seen new craters from fresh impacts on the surface!

However, the atmosphere is substantial enough to interact with the surface. Winds blow seasonally,filling craters with the ubiquitous dust. There's also sand on Mars, made of erodedbasaltic rock, so it's grey. The wind blows this into beautiful dunes, including seriesof parallel ridges in crater floors, and barchan or horseshoe-shaped dunes.

Mars also gets dust devils, towering vortices of wind similar to tornadoes. These dust devilshave been seen from orbit, and when they blow the red dust around on the greyish basalticplains, they can leave behind incredibly complex and beautiful curlicues.

One of my favorite recent discoveries about Mars is that it has avalanches! There arelots of cliffs towering above the surface, and in the spring, when buried frozen carbondioxide thaws, it can dislodge material, creating tremendous cascades of rock and dust. Severalof these have been caught in the act by orbiting space probes.

Mars has two moons: Small, potato-shaped rocks named Deimos and Phobos. Both are tiny; Phobosis about 25 kilometers across, and Deimos just 15. Both look very much like asteroids,and may indeed have been captured by Mars from the nearby asteroid belt.

To be honest,though, it's not clear what their origins are.

Phobos orbits Mars only 6000 km over the surface, and it moves so rapidly in its orbit that it orbits faster than Mars rotates; from the surface it appears to rise in the west andset in the east. Tides from Mars are altering its orbit, slowly lowering Phobos closer andcloser to the surface. In a few million years, it's expected to drop low enough to actuallyenter the atmosphere and impact the surface. That'll be really exciting to watch...from a safe distance.

Incidentally, from some locations on the surface, the moons can be seen to transit the Sun,passing directly across its face. The rovers on Mars have taken lots of pictures of theseevents, which is pretty cool.

So Mars has rocks, air, weather, and volcanoes... but what about water? If it has frozen waterat the poles, what about the rest of the planet?

We know there's water ice at the mid-latitudes of Mars; some recent small asteroid impactshave white area around them; underground deposits of ice splashed out by the impact. There'sno strong evidence of liquid water on the surface of Mars right now though. Some craterwalls collapse a bit and have dark channels running down them, which look like they could'vebeen carved by flowing water, but there are other possible sources too, so their cause still isn't certain.

But in the past, things were different. Mars was once very wet. There's tons of evidencefor flowing water on the surface long ago, including dry river beds, dry lakes, sedimentarylayers, and minerals we know need water to form. There's even evidence Mars had oceans.

But that's all gone now. What happened? It's not clear. Billions of years ago Marswas almost certainly warmer and had a thicker atmosphere. But for some reason, its internaldynamo shut down, and its magnetic field disappeared. This left it vulnerable to the solar wind,and over billions of years the Martian atmosphere was eroded away. The water went with it.

This raises another obvious question: If it had air and water, could it have had life?

That question wasn't taken terribly seriously just a few decades ago, but now we're veryinterested in it, enough to spend a lot of money sending probes to Mars to look at whatconditions for life are like now and once were in the past. It's still an open question,and we know life on Earth got its start not long after the surface cooled. Mars is smaller and cooled more quickly after its formation, so it's not crazy at all to wonder if lifeformed there, even before it did here.

Intriguingly, the Curiosity rover detected simple organic molecules in a rock sample—thisdoesn't mean there's life, but it means the ingredients were and are there. It alsodetected a brief spike in methane, a volatile gas that can be produced by life... as wellas by other, geologic processes. The evidence we have right now is maddeningly vague,but we're just starting out. Give it time!

Mars isn't the same planet it used to be. But that doesn't mean it's off limits.

Getting to Mars is hard—over half the missions sent there have failed—but not impossible.

Perseverance Rover on Mars

We've had amazing successes, including orbiters, landers, and rovers. I'd say we've learned as muchabout the Red Planet in the past couple of decades as we had in all the centuries of study before them.

Still, all we've sent are robots. They're good, and relatively inexpensive, but they'reslow. They can only cover so much ground. A human could do as much in a week as a rovercould in years... but humans are fragile. We need water, air, food; we aren't terribly tolerant of radiation or vacuum.

But the idea of sending people to Mars isn't as nuts as it might have once been. We'regetting better at building rockets, and the tech needed for human exploration of Marsis being developed now. There are even discussions about landing sites, and where to build bases.

One interesting idea is to use lava tubes—underground caverns created by ancient lava flows, wherethe top of the flow cooled and created a roof. We know these exist on

Mars because we'veseen holes in the roofs, called skylights, openings to the cavern below. This would provideshelter from solar radiation, protection from weather—Mars can get some pretty nasty duststorms in the spring—and could be sealed up and filled with air. From there, a lot of theplanet could be explored, and in a few years we'd once again dwarf everything we've learned up to that point.

I can't say when this'll happen—20 years from now, maybe 30 or more—but it'll happen.

Eventually, there will be life on Mars. And it'll be us.

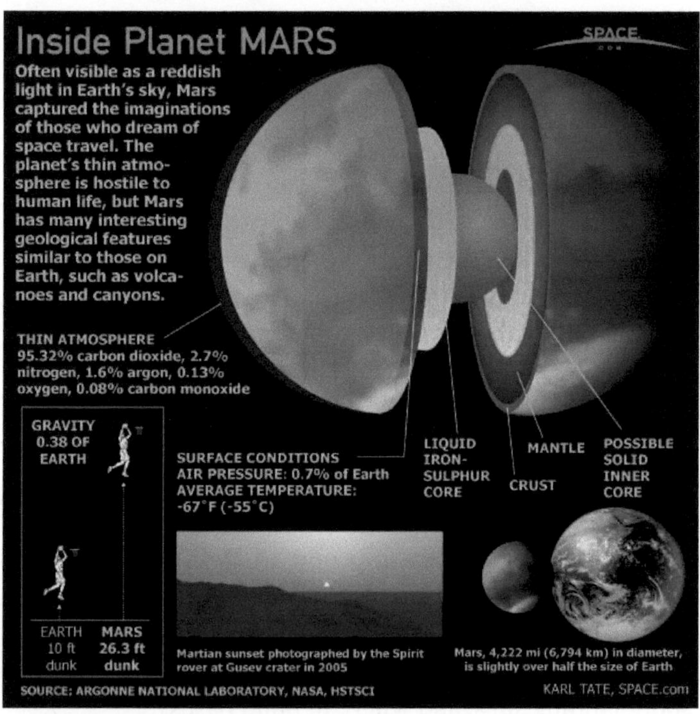

CHAPTER SIXTEEN

THE JUPITER

The Jupiter

Jupiter is the largest planet in the solar system. It's not even close: All the otherplanets could fit inside it with room to spare. It's a gas giant, which means it's gassy, and... giant.

And I do mean giant. It's 11 times wider than Earth—more than a thousand Earths couldfit inside it, and it has a mass over 300 times that of our planet. Despite its bulk, it rotates extremely rapidly: One day on Jupiter is a mere 10 hours long! That's the fastestspin of any of the planets in the solar system.

Not surprisingly, a planet that big can reflect a lot of sunlight, and even though it orbits the Sun on average at a distance of about 800 million kilometers, it's one of the brightest objects in the night sky.

With binoculars or a small telescope, Jupiter is a wonder. You can easily see it as a disk,and its four biggest moons are readily visible—if they weren't hidden by the planet's glare,they'd be naked eye objects. Galileo himself discovered those moons.

They're worlds in their own .

When we look at Jupiter we're not seeing its surface. We're seeing the tops of itsclouds, and they're a strange mix of permanence and change. The atmosphere of Jupiter is banded,with multiple stripes running parallel to its equator. The lighter-colored stripes arecalled zones, and the darker ones belts. They're fairly stable, though their shape and coloringchange over time.

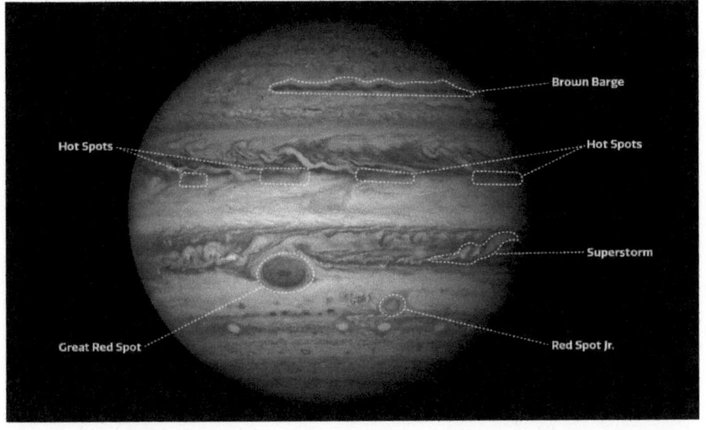

Jupiter

Belts and zones circulate around the planet in opposite directions. They form due to convectionin Jupiter's atmosphere. Upwelling air cools and forms white ammonia clouds; that createsthe light colored zones. That air flows to the sides and sinks, and sunlight changesthe chemistry in the clouds forming molecules that color the air yellow, red, and brown.

This is what causes the darker belts.

In May of 2010, one of Jupiter's biggest belts sank so deeply it disappeared from viewcompletely, covered by other clouds! Then, a few months later, it popped back up andreappeared, none the worse for wear. This has happened several times in the past, too.

Turbulence in the regions between zones and belts can create storms, gigantic vorticesraging in the clouds. Dozens of them dot the face of Jupiter all the time, but there isone to rule them all: the Great Red Spot, a fittingly huge storm for a giant planet.

It's actually a colossal hurricane, several times larger than our entire planet Earth,with sustained wind speeds of 500 kph. And it's old; it was first seen in the late17th century—imagine a storm on Earth lasting for more than three centuries! And it maybe far older; the 1600s is just when we first... spotted it.

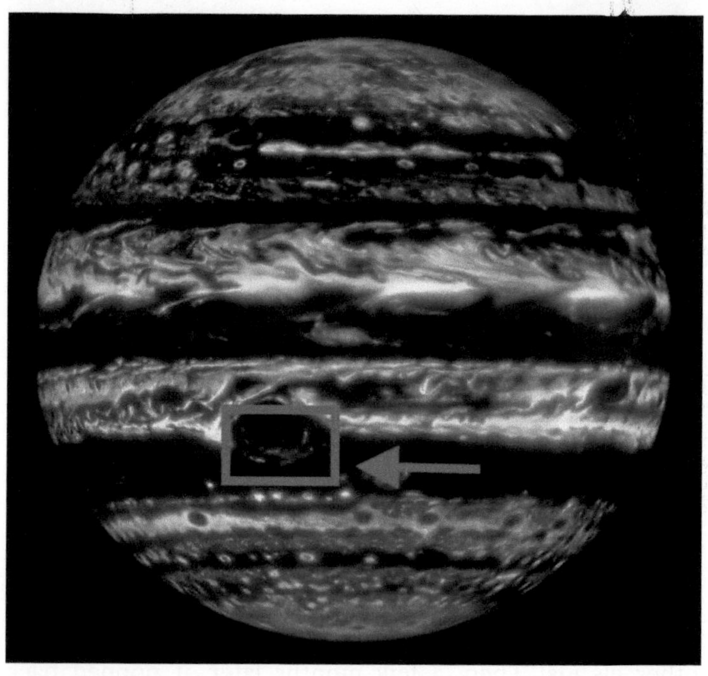

Great Red Spot

So, why is it so stable? It turns out that a vortex, a local spinning region in a fluid,can persist if the fluid in which it's embedded is itself rotating. Jupiter's rapid spin is what keeps the Red Spot circulating! And the redness is probably due to cyanide-likemolecules that absorb blue light, letting redder light pass through.

Weirdly, the Red Spot appears to be shrinking! It was substantially bigger and more elongatedjust a few decades ago. It changes color over time, too, having gone from deep red to salmonand then back again. No one knows why its shape, size, and color change, but given howlong the Spot's been around, I doubt it's going to evaporate any time soon.

Remember, we're only seeing the tops of the clouds on Jupiter. Its atmosphere is thick,several hundred kilometers deep! Like the composition of the Sun, the air on Jupiteris mostly hydrogen and helium, but it's also laced with ammonia, methane, and other poisonous gases.

As you dive into Jupiter's atmosphere, the pressure increases with depth. But you'll never reach the surface; the planet doesn't really have a proper surface. The gas getsthicker and hotter, and eventually just sort of smoothly changes into a liquid over a severalhundred km range below the clouds.

Below that is where things get really weird. Instead of a mantle, like terrestrial planets,Jupiter has a huge region made up of liquid metallic hydrogen. We think of hydrogen asbeing a gas, or, if it gets really cold, a liquid. But under the ridiculous pressuresgenerated deep inside Jupiter, hydrogen undergoes this strange transformation. Individual atoms don't hold on to their electrons, but instead share them. This means the hydrogen can conductelectricity, and has other properties more like a metal. This substance is hot, too:about 10,000° C, hotter than the surface of the Sun! If we could see it, it would glowtremendously bright.

Finally, at its center is most likely a dense core of material, probably composed of rockand metal. We really don't know, because it's incredibly difficult to understand the physics and chemistry of material locked in at those pressures and temperatures. What'sweirder is that we're not even sure if Jupiter has a core! If it did, it's possible itwas eroded away by currents of hot metallic hydrogen early on in Jupiter's formation process.

It's also possible it never had a core in the first place.

The solar system formed from a flat disk of gas and dust. The center of this disk is wherethe Sun was born, and it's thought that the planets formed as smaller particles ofmaterial stuck together during random collisions farther out in the disk. As they got bigger—much bigger—these protoplanets eventually started to grow even faster by drawing in materialaround them due to their gravity.

Jupiter formed where the disk was thick, rich with material. It's possible that severallarge protoplanets were forming, collided, and stuck together to really kickstart Jupiter'sgrowth. If that were the case, it started out with a rocky metallic core, and once itgot big enough it drew in that gas that made it the giant we see today.

Another idea is that Jupiter didn't grow from the bottom up, but from the top down:The disk itself collapsed in several places to form huge, distended clumps. These thenwould have collided, stuck, and created the planet. If that's the case, then Jupitermight not have a core at all.

The Jupiter

These two different mechanisms make different predictions about Jupiter's structure, andthat means that, hopefully, we can eventually figure out which is correct by studying Jupitermore carefully. But at the moment we still don't know.

Either way, Jupiter grew immense, and it's mostly liquid under all that atmosphere. Couplethat with its rapid rotation, and you can see it's noticeably flattened! It's widerat the equator than through the poles by about 6% due to centrifugal force.

So, Jupiter is a big bruiser of a planet. But how close was it to becoming a star?

Sometimes, people say Jupiter is a "failed star"; in other words, as it formed it almostgot massive enough that nuclear fusion could start in its center, turning it into a star.

When a star forms, hydrogen fusion starts when the star gathers so much mass that itsgravity can compress atoms together in its core hard enough to get them to fuse. Thishappens when a star has roughly $1/12^{th}$ of the Sun's mass. In fact, the smallest starswe see do have about that mass.

What about Jupiter? The mass of Jupiter is about $1/1000^{th}$ the mass of the Sun, far toolittle to undergo fusion in its core. If you want to turn Jupiter into a star, you'dhave a lot of work ahead of you: You'd have to take Jupiter... and then add about 80 moreJupiters to it!

Saying Jupiter is a failed star is really unfair. It's not a failed star. It's areally successful planet.

Even though Jupiter isn't a star, it does have another funny property: It emits moreheat than it receives from the Sun.

The Earth and other terrestrial, rocky planets are in a heat balance with the Sun; we emitpretty much the same amount of heat that we receive. But Jupiter is different. After it formed, it started to cool by radiating away heat from its upper atmosphere. A large fractionof the planet is gas, remember, and when you cool a gas in contracts. So the atmospherecools and contracts, but this increases the pressure inside the planet, so it heats up!

That heat works its way out of Jupiter, and gets radiated away as infrared light. In theend, the amount of heat Jupiter gives off is more than it receives from the Sun.

It's still actively cooling, 4.5 billion years after it formed! Oh and hey, remember thebelts and zones, the stripes we see in Jupiter's atmosphere, and all the storms that pop up?

Those are driven in large part by Jupiter's internal heat. On Earth our weather is poweredby heat from the Sun, but on Jupiter they get their energy from the planet itself!

Jupiter has a very strong magnetic field, no doubt due to all of that metallic hydrogeninside it coupled with its rapid rotation. Like Earth it has aurorae at its poles asthe solar wind is funneled down to the cloud tops.s, Jupiter'smoons affect the magnetic field and aurorae on Jupiter as well.

Jupiter also has a ring, though it's not nearly as grand as Saturn's. It wasn'teven discovered until we sent space probes to the planet. The ring is made of dust, probably thrown into orbit around the planet due to meteorite impacts on its smaller moons.

Speaking of impacts, we know that Earth gets hit by interplanetary debris all the time:Go outside for an hour and you're bound to see a few meteors. Jupiter, being larger and with more gravity, gets hit a lot more. A lot. A lot more. And sometimes it gets hellaciouslywhacked. In 1994, the comet Shoemaker-Levy 9 impacted Jupiter. Multiple times: Jupiter's fierce gravitational tides had ripped the comet into dozens of pieces, and each slammed into the planet one after the other with the force of millions of nuclear weapons. Thescars left in the upper atmosphere from the plumes of material that exploded outward lasted for months.

Several smaller impacts have been seen in Jupiter's atmosphere since then, and itmay suffer an impact large enough to see from Earth every year or so.

And while that sounds scary, it might actually be our savior. There's an idea that Jupiter'sgravity tends to take comets that fall toward the inner solar system and fling them awayinto interstellar space. Over the eons, this has cleaned out a lot of otherwise dangerousobjects that could have eventually hit Earth. On the other hand, Jupiter has a tendencyto warp the orbits of some other comets so that they do swing by the Earth. It's hardto say if Jupiter's influence is a net benefit or not.

But either way, it's clearly the 2 septillion ton gorilla in the solar system.

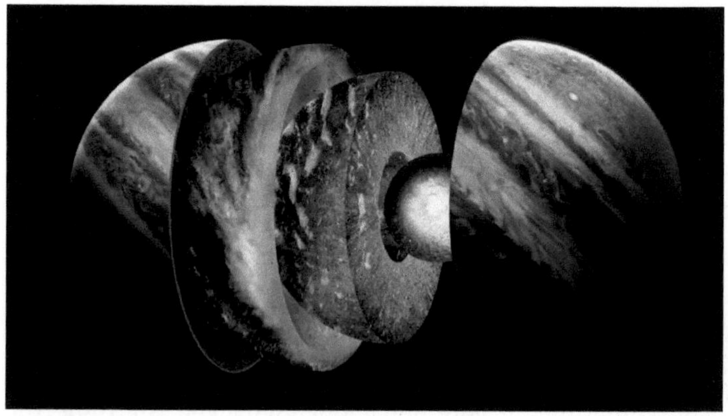

Interior Of Jupiter

CHAPTER SEVENTEEN

THE JUPITER'S MOONS

Jupiter's Moon (Io)

As we read in the last , Jupiter is by far the largest and most massive planetin the solar system. That means it has a very strong gravitational field, which also meansit can hold on to a lot of moons. A lot. Right now, there are 79 that havebeen confirmed. And how many it really has depends on how small an object you're willing to call a "moon."

In 1610, Galileo pointed his telescope at Jupiter, and witnessed a revolution. Oh, hey, literally!

He saw three little stars lined up on either side of Jupiter, stars he could not see withhis naked eye.

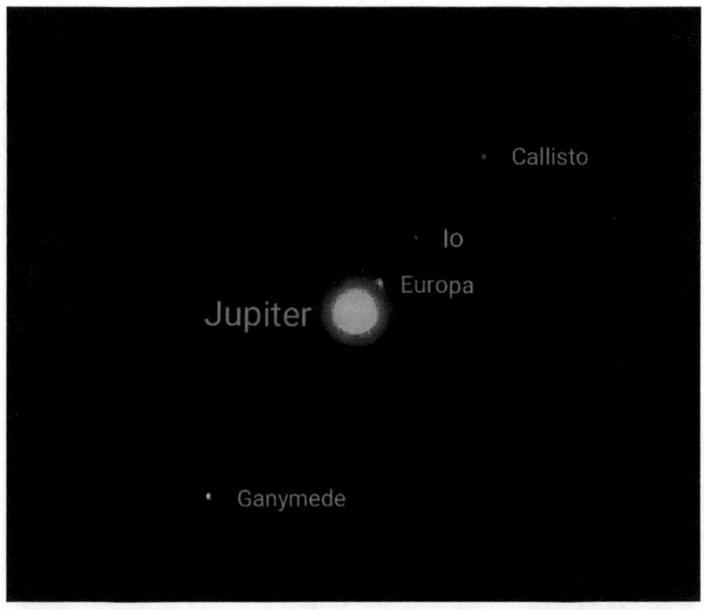

Enter Caption

And they moved! A week later he saw a fourth one, and he knew he was seeingobjects revolving, orbiting around Jupiter. It was proof that not everything in the solar system revolved around the Earth. That was a pretty big deal.

Those four moons are now called the Galilean moons in his honor. Not bad for a week's work.

All four are really big, too. If Jupiter weren't there, drowning them out with its glare, they'dbe visible to the naked eye. In that case we might even call them planets, too.

The biggest of Jupiter's moons is Ganymede. At 5270 km across, it's the biggest moonof any planet. It's even bigger than the planet Mercury—in fact, in size it's halfwaybetween Mercury and Mars!

Callisto

The surface is heavily cratered, and there's no indication of any volcanoes or tectonicactivity. That means the surface is very old, maybe as old as Callisto itself. It even hasan atmosphere, but it's a tad thin: roughly one one-hundred-billionth the pressure ofEarth's air at the surface!

Callisto orbits Jupiter farthest out of the four biggies, almost 2 million km away. That'stoo far to gravitationally interact with the other three; when I talk about the moons affectingeach other, it's really the other three interacting.

Next up is Io. It's only a little bit bigger than our own Moon, and orbits Jupiter so tightlyit only takes about a day and a half to go around the planet.

Io

When the Voyager 1 space probe passed Io in 1979 it revealed a surface that was reallyweird. It was yellow and orange and red and black, and didn't seem to have any obviousimpact craters. An engineer, Linda Morabito, noticed that in one image there appeared tobe what looked like another moon behind Io, partially eclipsed by it. But that was nomoon: It was a volcano on Io erupting, its plume shooting up from the surface and openingup into a wide arc.

Enter Caption

Io is the most volcanic object in the entire solar system, with over 400 active volcanoes.

Quite a few of them are erupting at any given time, and images taken even a few months apartshow changes in the surface due to ejected material. A lot of the erupted material isrich in sulphur, which is why the surface has all those odd colours on it.

The energy for all this activity comes from the other moons: As they pass Io in theirorbits they flex it via tides, heating its interior through friction.

A lot of that sulphur ends up as a very thin atmosphere around Io, and some of those sulphuratoms are then picked up by Jupiter's powerful magnetic field as it sweeps past Io and acceleratesthem to very high speeds. This has created a tremendous donut-shaped radiation belt aroundJupiter, like Earth's Van Allen belts, but far more powerful. The radiation there isso intense it would kill an unprotected human in minutes. Of course, if you're floatingin space near Jupiter unprotected, you might have some more immediate concerns.

Enter Caption

Oh, one more thing: Both Ganymede and Io are magnetically connected to Jupiter. Charged particles flow from those moons along the lines of magnetism to Jupiter, which thenslams them down at Jupiter's poles, just like the Earth does with the particles fromthe solar wind. On Earth this creates the aurorae, the northern and southern lights,and it does at Jupiter, too. You can even see the ultraviolet glow where each of the moons connects to Jupiter; their magnetic footprints in the planet's atmosphere!

And, now we come to Europa, the smallest but perhaps most exciting of all the Galileanmoons. Slightly smaller than our moon, it was known for decades to be very reflective, meaningits surface was probably loaded with water ice. But even so, the Voyager observations were shocking.

Europa

They showed a surface completely lacking in craters, meaning something had resurfacedthe moon like Io or Venus; but Europa has no volcanoes. Even more intriguing, the surfacewas covered in long cracks, dark streaks all over the moon, as well as complex ridges.

These and other features appear to be due to material from the interior of Europa wellingup and forming the new surface, kind of like the way lava does on Earth.

But in this case, the material is water. It's now thought that Europa has an entire oceanof water, sealed up under a solid crust of ice several kilometers thick. Water wellingup and moving under the crust causes it to shift, creating all the various surface features.

The amount of water that may be locked up on Europa is staggering; easily more thanall the water in all the oceans on Earth! Like Ganymede and Io, the interior of Europais kept warm by tidal flexing from the other moons, keeping the ice melted.

Now get this: A lot of Europa's material is silicate rock, like on Earth and otherterrestrial planets, located in a layer under the ocean. If this interacts with the oceanin the same way Earth's oceans interact with the sea floor, this could make the subsurfaceEuropan water salty. In fact, those dark cracks on the surface have been found to be richin salt and organic materials - in other words, carbon-based compounds!

This is pretty exciting. We think Earth's life originated in salty ocean water. If thereare carbon-based molecules actually in Europa's water, it's not too crazy to wonder if thesame spark that occurred here also happened there. We think Europa has everything it needsto spawn life. We just don't have any direct evidence of it yet.

Some people have proposed sending a space probe to Europa specifically to look for life.

It would land near a crack in the ice, where the crust is thinner, and somehow penetrate it(perhaps melting its way down). Chemical sampling could then look for signs of biological activity.

That's amazing ,: The idea of life in Europa, even if it's just microbial life,is taken very seriously by astrobiologists, scientists who study the possibility of lifein space. It used to be science fiction. Now it's a topic of scholarly research.

Astronomers have a concept called the habitable zone: The distance a planet can be from its parent star where the temperature on the planet's surface can support liquid water. It's afuzzy concept; Venus and Mars are both technically in the Sun's habitable zone, but Venus istoo hot and Mars too cold for liquid water. Atmospheres make a big difference. But it'sstill a useful concept as rule of thumb for potential habitability.

But Europa changed that. Jupiter is way, way outside the Sun's habitable zone, yet there'sEuropa, all wet. It's a great example that we need to let our ideas breathe a bit sometimes,let them relax and flow outside the boundaries we set for them. When we look for signs of

life on planets orbiting other stars, I bet we'll have to keep our minds open to typesof life we've never considered before.

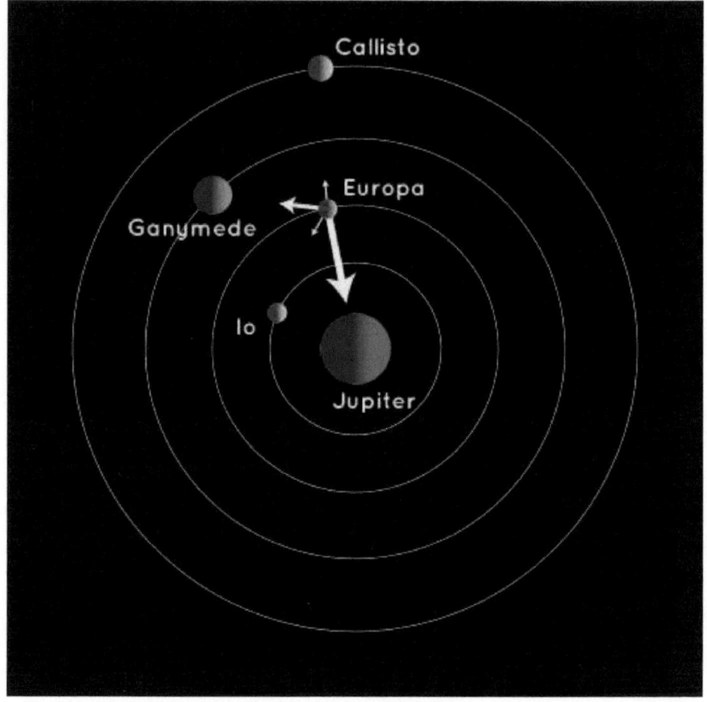

Enter Caption

Those are just the four big moons of Jupiter, each thousands of kilometers across. Theyprobably formed along with Jupiter, coalescing from the eddies and whorls around the protoJupiteras it formed billions of years ago.

But the planet has dozens of other moons, too. About the only thing they all have incommon is that they're tidally locked to Jupiter; they all rotate once for every time they go around the planet. Jupiter's tides are hundreds of times stronger than Earth's,so no surprise there.

The next biggest moon after The Big Four is way smaller; named Amalthea, it's an irregularlump about 250 km across its longest dimension. It was discovered in 1892, and it's red—probablypolluted by sulfur from Io. It orbits just over 100,000 km from Jupiter's cloudtops;if you stood on Amalthea's surface, Jupiter would fill half the sky.

The moons get smaller and more irregularly shaped from there, with Himalia and Thebeand Elara and Pasiphae, down to Hegemone, Kale, and Kallichore, which are no bigger than hills.

Many of the irregular, distant moons of Jupiter orbit the planet backwards relative to theothers, in what are called retrograde orbits. They may be captured asteroids from the nearbyasteroid belt. Many of the moons have orbital characteristics that are very similar, too,which may indicate they were once a single object that broke up. Several such families of moons orbit Jupiter.

The smallest moons we've seen are roughly a kilometer across. If they were sitting onEarth they might be hard to pedal up on a bicycle, but orbiting Jupiter they hardlyrate as more than debris. There are probably thousands of moons the size of houses circling the planet, and who knows, maybe millions the size of tennis balls.

Should we even call those moons? Maybe. But I don't really worry about that kind ofthing. The important thing to remember is that these are worlds, big and small, eachfascinating, rich, and diverse. And there's still a lot more left to explore about them.

CHAPTER EIGHTEEN

THE SATURN

The Saturn

So now we've come to the last of the naked eye planets in the solar system: Saturn. It'sthe second largest planet, but ironically the least dense. In fact, if you could finda bathtub big enough, Saturn would float in it!

But it would leave a ring.

OK, that's the oldest joke in astronomy, but it's true. Saturn is a gas giant, whichmeans it has a thick atmosphere. Like Jupiter, it probably has a rocky core several timesthe mass of Earth, surrounded by layers of ice and weird, metallic hydrogen. On top of all that is its atmosphere, hundreds of kilometers deep, composed mostly of hydrogen, with asmaller amount of helium and a whole bunch of trace gases like methane and ammonia.

Overall, its density is about 2/3rds that of water. It wouldn't really float, though;its gravity would draw in all the water from the giant bathtub... although, actually, cometo think of it, a bathtub filled with water big enough to put Saturn in would have more

mass than the planet, so the water would pull Saturn in.

Astronomy is fun!

Saturn spins really quickly, completing a day in just ten and a half hours. Its rapidrotation and low density means it's really oblate, or squished; it's 10% wider throughthe Equator than through the poles! That's really noticeable through a telescope.

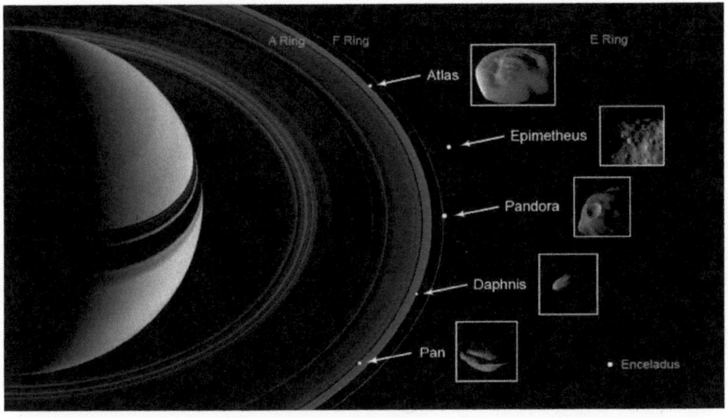

Saturn

When we look at Saturn, we only see its cloud tops. Those clouds are mostly ammonia ices,with water clouds lower down. The atmosphere is banded, like Jupiter's, but the patternis much fainter, probably due to Saturn being farther from the Sun and therefore colder,as well as the atmosphere being deeper than Jupiter's too.

That's not to say Saturn doesn't have storms. Oval hurricanes pop up every now andagain, and in 2010 a huge storm erupted in Saturn's northern hemisphere. It was discoveredby an amateur astronomer, and Cassini spacecraft pictures showed it getting so big it literallywrapped around the planet, reaching a length of over 300,000 kilometers!

Traces of it persisted for years.

One of the most striking features on Saturn is a huge, hexagonal vortex at its north pole.

Vortices like this are common on planets; Earth and Venus have them too. That well-definedsix-sided shape is pretty freaky, but it's actually a natural outcome of a spinning fluid—theair circulating Saturn's atmosphere—which itself is in a spinning system—in this case,the planet itself. It's not that different than Earth's jet stream, but it's a lotbigger, about 20,000 kilometers across... wider than Earth. And right at its center,over Saturn's north pole, is a ridiculously beautiful storm system about 2000 kilometersacross. Wind speeds there have been clocked at 500 kilometers per hour.

Storm on Saturn (Rose)

Saturn as a planet is of course an amazing place, but c'mon. When you think Saturn,you think rings. As well you should.

Saturn's rings were seen by Galileo, but his telescope lacked the resolution to reallyfigure out what they were—he thought Saturn might be three objects in close proximity.

Some decades later the Dutch scientist Christiaan Huygens correctly interpreted their appearanceas a ring surrounding the planet.

They're not solid. If they were they'd get torn apart, since the inner edge wouldorbit the planet way faster than the outer edge. They're actually made of countless small chunks of very nearly pure water ice. Each particle orbits the planet independently...so I guess Saturn wins in the "which planet has the most moons" category.

What really gets me about Saturn's rings is their scale. They're 250,000 kilometersacross. If you put Saturn between the Earth and Moon, the rings would cover ⅔ that distance.

And yet, despite their size, they're incredibly thin: They average about ten meters thick.

That's amazing. That's thinner, to scale, than a sheet of paper. Way thinner: If youshrank Saturn down to the size of a piece of paper, that paper would be ten thousand times thicker than the rings.

So yeah, Saturn's rings are flat. But why?

Well that's tied to their origin, though the specifics of how they came to be aren'texactly known. One idea is that they were originally an icy moon that got disruptedby a huge collision. The shattered moon particles would have spread around Saturn, and any ofthem that were on a tilted orbit would quickly collide with others, and in the end that would average out all their orbits to form a flattened ring.

Or maybe there was once a large moon near Saturn, that was big enough to be differentiated;that means the rocky bits fell to the moon's core, while the ice stayed near the surface.

As it plowed through the material around the protoSaturn, the moon's icy layer got strippedoff, forming the rings. And again, that would form a very flat disk.

However they formed, collisions would quickly flatten the ring out. And remember, Saturnis oblate, so as the rings formed they would've felt a gravitational tug from Saturn's equatorialbulge, centering them right over the planet's midline.

Saturn has three main rings, give or take. In classic imaginative astronomer fashion,they're given the names A,

B, and C—in order of their discovery. B is the broadest, roughly 26,000 kilometers wide. A is outside B, while the C ring is fainter and inside the B ring.

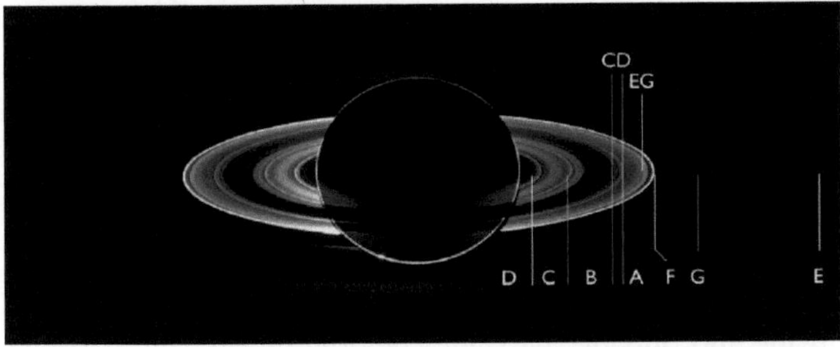

Saturn's Rings

When the rings were first observed, the A and B rings were thought to be one ring. But then the Italian astronomer Giovanni Domenico Cassini discovered a gap between them, andwe now call that the Cassini Division. It's about 5000 kilometers across, but it's notempty! There are quite a few very narrow rings inside of it.

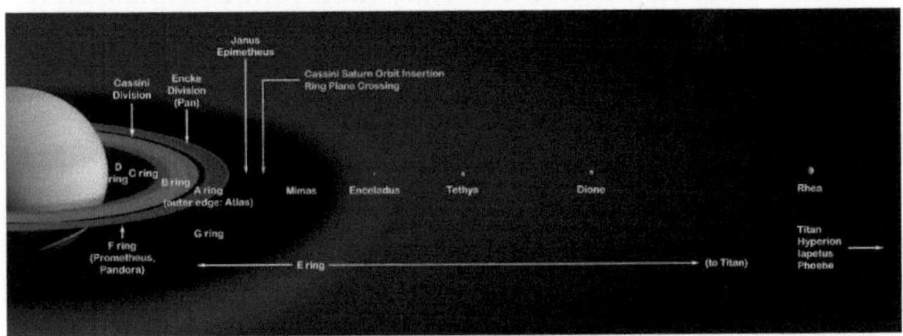

Saturn's Rings

The gap is due to one of Saturn's moons, Mimas. If you're an ice particle in the Cassini division, you orbit Saturn twice for every one time Mimas goes around. This is called a resonance, and it means that the particles at that location get tugged repeatedlyby the gravity of Mimas, which in essence yanks them out of their orbit.

There are quite a few gaps in the rings caused by moons; in fact, there are hundreds of "ringlets" in the main rings. Even weirder, the F ring is outside the A ring, and is very narrow,just a few hundred kilometers across. It's kept that way by two moons, Prometheus andPandora, orbiting just inside and outside the ring. They tug on the ring particles insuch a way that keeps them confined to very strict orbits; if a particle wanders out, the moons' gravity drags it back in.

As the moons and ring particles interact, they can also create weird rippling wavesin the rings. : when small moons orbit Saturn on slightly inclinedorbits; it can create waves in the rings, tremendous vertical excursions that can reach several kilometers high.

Saturn is weird.

And so are its moons. I already mentioned Mimas, an icy moon that carves out the CassiniDivision with its gravity. It also suffered a massive impact long ago that created a singlehuge crater, making it look somehow familiar.

Saturn's Moons

But Saturn has two moons specifically you should know about. The first is Titan, a monster satellite that's actually bigger than Mercury, not that much smaller than Mars, and secondin moon size ranking only to Jupiter's moon Ganymede. Titan not only has a substantialatmosphere—the only moon to have one—but it's thicker than our air on Earth! I wouldn't suggest breathing it, though: It's mostly nitrogen, with a smattering of methane andhydrogen. It's also a hundred and eighty below zero Celsius there.

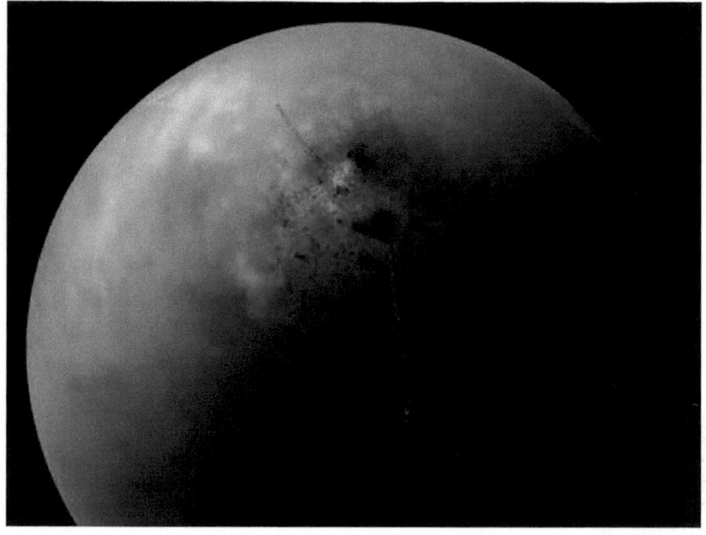

Titan

Titan's atmosphere has a thick layer of haze that prevents us from seeing the surfaceusing visible light. But using infrared and radar, though, the Cassini spacecraft, whichhas been orbiting Saturn since 2004, is able to map the surface. It also deployed a probe named Huygens to land on Titan's surface, the first time humanity had ever landed onan outer solar system moon.

What they saw was an odd world, Earth-like in some ways, and very alien in many others.

Titan has wind-sculpted dunes, but they're made of hydrocarbon grains, not sand. Thereare hints of volcanoes that spew liquid water instead of lava. These are called cryovolcanoes,cold volcanoes. This, together with measurements of Titan's gravitationalfield, have scientists thinking that Titan may have an underground ocean of liquid water.

Intriguingly, Titan also has long, winding channels indicating flows of some kind ofliquid on its surface. But it can't be water; it's far too cold on the surface for that.

So what kind of liquid could it be? Well, Cassini also spotted quite a few flat regionsnear Titan's north and south poles. These have since been confirmed to be lakes of liquidmethane—the first time any liquid has been seen on the surface of another world. Theshorelines of the lakes appear to change over time, too, hinting very strongly that Titanhas weather, driven by methane as opposed to water here on Earth.

Weather, atmosphere, surface liquids, and an abundance of organic, carbonbased molecules...could there be life on Titan? The conditions there are...interesting. We obviously don'tknow yet, but it's an exciting possibility.

And it's not the only Saturnian moon scientists are looking at for signs of life. Enceladusis a smaller, icy moon about 500 km across.. Enceladus is incredibly shiny, reflecting nearly all the light that hits it: a strong indicator it's covered in water ice.

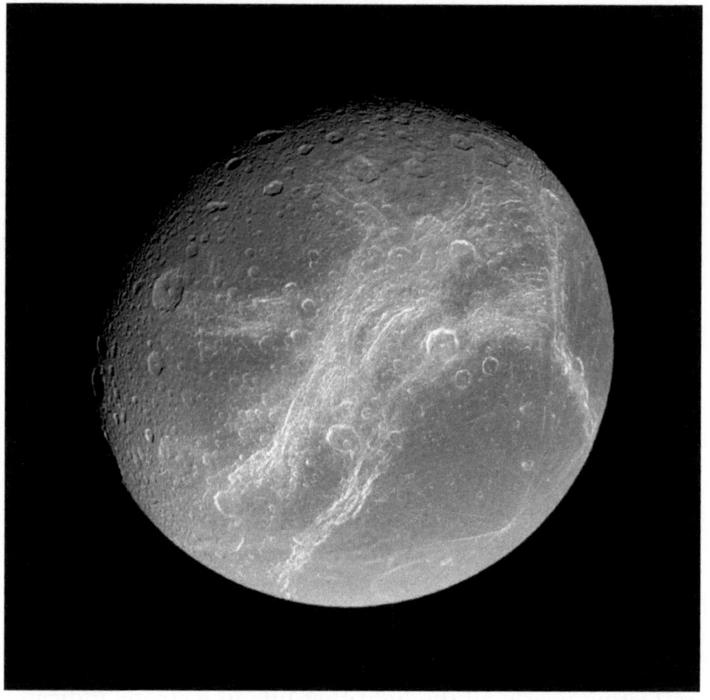

Enceladus

Parts of it are cratered, but other parts are very smooth, indicating some event resurfacedthe moon. The surface also has an extensive series of cracks in it, much like Jupiter'smoon Europa. Scientists suspected cryovolcanism, and that was confirmed quite dramatically in 2005 when Cassini spotted active geysers of water spewing from the south pole of Enceladus!

The water is erupting from a series of cracks nicknamed "tiger stripes", and is comingfrom deep under the surface. Like Europa, Enceladus has an undersurface ocean, keptliquid by Saturn's ferocious tides, which squeeze the moon as it orbits the planet.

The plumes reach several hundred kilometers from the moon's surface, and Cassini evenflew directly through the plumes, and detected organic molecules.

Could Enceladus be yet another harbor for life in the solar system? Again, no one knows,but I'd put it in the top three places to look, including Europa and Titan. It's weird,isn't it? We've always looked for planets where conditions were like here on Earth, but it turns out extremely cold moons may be the best places to seek out new life.

Saturn's Moon (Rhea)

Saturn has a huge retinue of other moons, too, and they're all pretty weird. Iapetusis shaped like a walnut, with a tall ridge of mountains encircling its equator; no one'squite sure how that formed. Hyperion looks like a huge piece of Styrofoam that's beenhit repeatedly with a BB gun—and that's not a bad analogy, since it has such a lowdensity it's likely to be extremely porous, like a sponge. A lot of Saturn's moons orbitthe planet backwards, retrograde; similar to several moons of Jupiter. These may be captured asteroids, or even Kuiper Belt Objects.. All in all, Saturn has over 60 moons we've discovered so far.

When you ask astronomers or astronauts what got them started, what was the very first thing that happened to them to inspire them to do what they do,overwhelmingly they will tell you: "I saw Saturn through a telescope."

Saturn is the crown jewel of the solar system. It's the best kind of astronomical object:Visually stunning, artistically gorgeous, and filled to overflowing with incredible science.

Saturn's Moon (Tethy)

CHAPTER NINETEEN

THE URANUS AND THE NEPTUNE

The Uranus

There are five planets in our solar system you can see without a telescope; well, sixif you include the one you're sitting on. But there are two more big ones out there,orbiting the Sun out in the cold depths of the outer solar system: Uranus and Neptune.

They're a lot alike in many ways, but of course they have their individual quirks.

Uranus was the first planet to be discovered, and by that I mean it wasn't known in ancient times. It took an astronomer with a telescope to find it. In 1781, William

Herschel wasmapping the skies through his telescope when he spotted a greenish object that was clearlya disk and not a dot, like a star. He noted its position, and moved on. But when he went to observe it again sometime later, he was astonished to discover it had moved!

It was quickly determined to be a planet, more distant from the Sun than Saturn. Intrue brown-nosing style, he named it Georgium Sidus, or George's star, after the reigning king George III. Yeah, happily, that name didn't stick, and keeping with the nomenclatureof Roman gods, the new planet was dubbed Uranus.

It actually is visible to the unaided eye if you have very sharpeyesight and very dark skies. It's right on the thin hairy edge of visibility. What'sfunny is that several people had observed it before Herschel, but none had noticed itsmovement. Some even catalogued it on their maps as a star!

The planet is massive—about 14.5 times the mass of Earth—but not terribly dense. Thismeans its interior must be made of lightweight stuff. Scientific models of the planet based on physicsand chemistry of the outer solar system indicate its interior is probably made up of three general layers.

There's a small rocky core, smaller than Earth, surrounded by a very thick layer ofmaterials like water, ammonia and methane. This mantle makes up the bulk of the planet,in fact, and is dense, hot, and under a lot of pressure. In many ways, it's more likean ocean than anything else. However, somewhat confusingly I'll admit, outer solar systemplanetary scientists refer to water, ammonia, and methane as "ice," so even though it's notice like we usually think of it here on Earth, we say that the mantle of Uranus is "icy."

To distinguish it from the gas giants Jupiter and Saturn, Uranus is called an “ice giant.”

Speaking of “ice,” here’s a really weird thing: Studies have shown that the pressureinside Uranus can break up methane molecules, squeezing the carbon in them so tightly thatit actually forms diamonds! These would then fall down to the base of the mantle like sparklyhailstones. Except it’s dark. But still, down there in the depths of Uranus there mayeven be an ocean of liquid diamonds, where solid ones float.

Not that we’ll ever see that. When we observe the planet, we’re only seeing the top ofits atmosphere. Besides hydrogen and helium, the air there is about 2% methane. Methaneis really good at absorbing red light, which means the light we see reflected from Uranus is mostly greenand blue, making the planet look distinctly cyan or aquamarine. And it’s pretty striking through a telescope.

But in visible light the planet looks almost featureless. It doesn’t have that deep bandinglike Jupiter, or even the pale ones of Saturn, though when you look in the infrared somebanding can be seen.

There are clouds, but again they’re difficult to see in visible light. The clouds are madeof methane, ammonia, and hydrogen sulphide—that last one is what makes rotten eggs smell so bad.

In late 2014, a bunch of storms popped up in Uranus’s atmosphere, so big and bright they were easily visible from Earth. The storms may have dredged up very reflective methaneice from lower down in the atmosphere -- and this time, I do mean icy ice -- which is whythey were bright. The northern hemisphere of Uranus is approaching summertime, which may be why these storms formed.

And that brings us to the weirdest thing about this planet: It's sideways!

If you were above the Earth's north pole looking down, you'd see our planet spinningcounter-clockwise, west to east. The Sun spins that way, and all the planets do as well...except Venus and Uranus. While Venus is flipped all the way over, Uranus is tilted by about98°. That means that in the summer, its axis is pointed almost directly at the Sun, soseasons on Uranus are pretty extreme, by outer solar system standards. Weird.

No one knows why Uranus is tipped so much. An obvious thought is that it got whacked, hard, by an impact long ago. If it were a grazing collision by a BIG object, that couldhave pushed hard enough on the planet to tip it over.

Unfortunately, Uranus is very far away, and has only been visited by spacecraft once—Voyager2, in 1986—and even then it was a quick flyby. Uranus's weird tilt is just one ofthose many mysteries that astronomers are trying to solve with limited data.

Uranus has a magnetic field, but it's truly odd: Its axis is tipped by over 50° fromthe planet's spin axis, and it's way off-center; the center of the magnetosphere is about 8000km from the planet's center. It may be that the magnetic field is generated in the icymantle, or that the core somehow interferes with the magnetic field, throwing it off.

Truthfully, no one really knows why.

Uranus has more than two dozen moons; five big ones and a bunch of dinkier ones.

Cool fact: The moons are named after characters in Shakespeare plays. So we have Ariel, Umbriel, Titania, Oberon, and Miranda. Even Puck!

Of them all, I think the most interesting one is Miranda. When Voyager 2 flew past,it revealed an icy world that looks like it was put together by Dr. Frankenstein: a patchworkof jumbled terrains all crammed together, criss-crossed by canyons and grooves. It'spossible a giant impact in its past actually disrupted the moon somewhat, and it settledback together into this weird mishmash.

But the reason I like it so much is a feature called Verona Rupes: It's the tallest cliffin the solar system, 5 to 10 kilometers high. If you jumped off the top, it would take yousix minutes to fall to the surface! That would be a fantastic ride.

Like Jupiter and Saturn, Uranus has a ring system, too. They were discovered by accidentin 1997; astronomers were observing Uranus pass directly in front of a star. They were hoping to use this to gather information about the planet's atmosphere as starlight passedthrough it. But they saw several dips in starlight before the main event, which they realizedwere from rings around the planet.

The rings are made of dark particles, probably ice and reddish organic molecules. There are13 rings known, most of them are very faint and narrow. They may have been created by an impact completely shattering a small moon orbiting Uranus, but as for now, the ring origins are unclear.

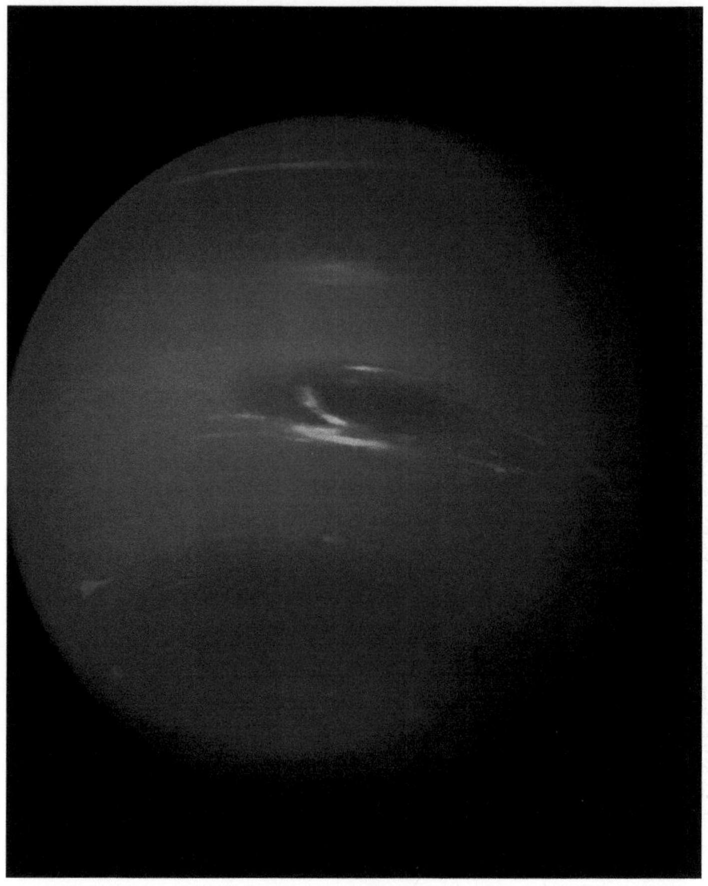

The Neptune

And then, finally, we have Neptune, the guardian of the solar system's nether regions. Neptune is an ice giant, like Uranus, and has a lot of similarities. Like its green brother, itprobably has a rocky core surrounded by a thick icy mantle of water, ammonia, and methane.

Above that is an atmosphere of hydrogen, helium, and methane.

But there are differences, too. Neptune is more massive than Uranus; 17 times Earth'smass, versus just 14.5 for Uranus. Neptune is slightly smaller than Uranus, which meansit's a lot denser. Also, while Uranus is teal, Neptune is a deep, rich azure—I liketo call it "the other blue planet", the first one being, y'know, Earth. Througha telescope, Neptune's color is quite lovely. It has roughly the same amount of red-light-absorbingmethane in its atmosphere, as Uranus does. So its deeper blue hue is something of a mystery.

That may have to do with its active atmosphere. Unlike blander Uranus, Neptune has cloudsof methane, ammonia, and hydrogen sulfide lying the skies at different depths, and whitestreaky clouds were seen during the Voyager 2 flyby in 1989. They looked whipped by wind,and for good reason: Sustained wind speeds in Neptune's atmosphere have been clockedat over 2000 kph: Faster than the speed of sound on Earth! It's thought that the lowtemperatures in the atmosphere reduce friction, allowing the winds to gather to such amazing speeds.

Voyager saw a huge storm marring Neptune's face, called—the Great Dark Spot. A few years later, when Hubble was used to observe the planet, the spot wasgone, but others had appeared. They're probably vortices, cyclones, which allow us to seethrough the upper atmosphere and peer farther into Neptune's depths.

Neptune has a magnetic field, and like Uranus, it's offset from the planet's center.

Perhaps that icy mantle is at work, somehow interfering with the generation of the magneticfields in both planets.

Neptune has rings, too.. There are three main rings; two narrowand one broad. They're clumpy, and have bright stretches that make the rings lookmore like incomplete arcs. It's possible those arcs are being constrained by small moon-lets near the rings.

Speaking of which, Neptune has over a dozen known moons. Most are quite small, but one,Triton, is by far the largest. At 2700 kilometers across it's smaller than our own Moon, butthe rest of them are really dinky. Triton orbits around Neptune backwards, retrograde.

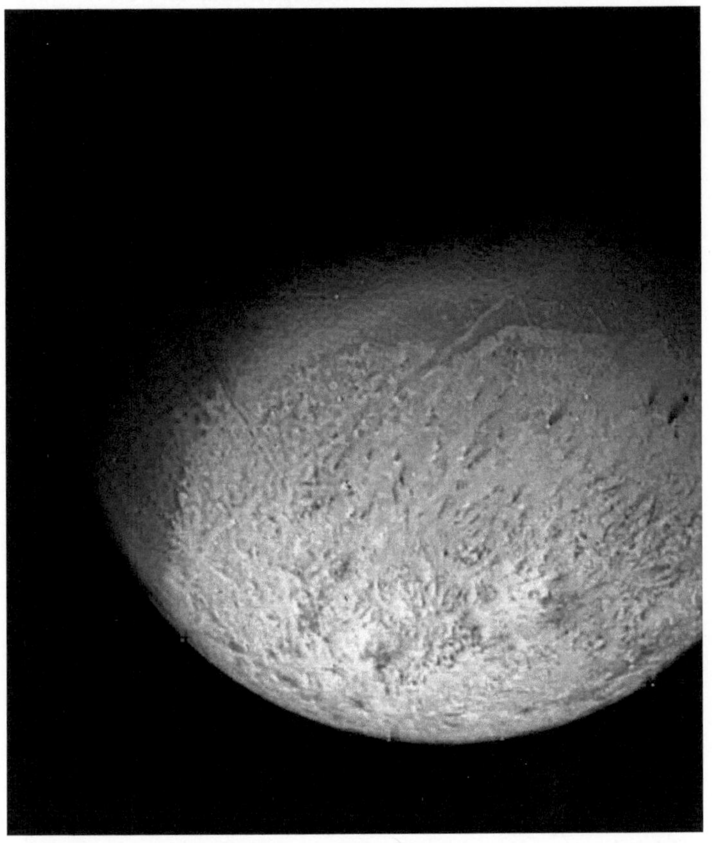

Triton

There's a repository of giant iceballs out past Neptune,so Triton was probably one of those that got too close to Neptune and was captured by its gravity.

Most of what we know about Triton came from a single flyby of Voyager 2 in 1989, and onlyabout 40% of the surface was seen. But this quick glimpse revealed a weird little moon.

The surface is covered in nitrogen ice, as well as water and carbon dioxide ice. It'sreally flat, and has very few craters, meaning something resurfaced it in geologically recenttimes. Most likely this was from cryovolcanoes, cold volcanism; that is, volcanoes where waterand ammonia take the place of lava there.

Also, Triton has been seen to have active geysers of nitrogen erupting from its surface!

They're probably due to warming from the Sun, and they make Triton one of the few objectsin the solar system seen to be geologically active. It also has a very thin atmosphereof nitrogen, probably due to evaporation from the surface.

After all this, Neptune is special in another way, too.

Neptune is faint, and can only be seen telescopically. It was discovered in 1846, and it wasn't an accident. Over the decades, astronomers observed Uranus, and found something weird, It wasn't where it was supposed to be. Over time, its predicted position was off fromwhere it actually was. The French mathematician Urbain Le Verrier concluded that this wasdue to an unseen planet, and was able to use the mathematics of orbital mechanics to predictwhere the new planet would be. He sent a letter with the predicted position to the BerlinObservatory. Astronomer Johann Galle read the letter, when right out and found the planetthat very night. Neptune was within a degree of the predicted spot.

Amazingly, another mathematician, Englishman John Couch Adams, had also worked on the mathand had made a similar prediction -- but Le Verrier beat him by two days.

Two. Days. Of such tight races are fame made in science.

Interestingly, over time, Neptune seemed to wander from its predicted position as well.

The Pluto

A ninth massive planet was predicted, leading to a grand search that resulted in the discovery of Pluto. But Pluto was far too small to affect Neptune. When Voyager passed both Uranus andNeptune, it found the masses of the planets were different than what had been measuredfrom Earth. When the new masses were used in the orbital equations, Uranus and Neptune were rightwhere they were supposed to be. It helps to have the right numbers to plug into your equations.

Pluto, therefore, was found by accident. That meansNeptune is the only planet in the solar system found via math.

See? Your algebra teacher was right: Someday this stuff will be important.

CHAPTER TWENTY

THE ASTEROID BELT

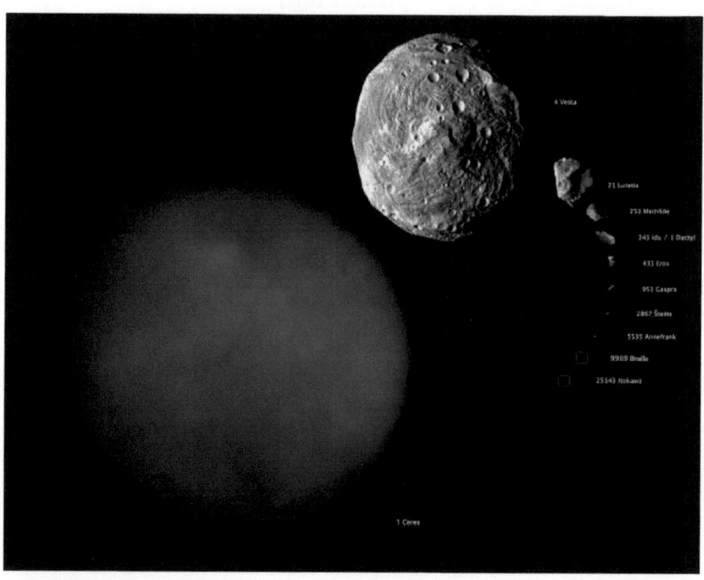

Asteroids

When you look at a diagram of the solar system, you'll see a big gap between Mars and Jupiter.

A few centuries ago, that gap bugged astronomers; they really wanted there to be a planet in there.

On the first day of the 19th century—January 1, 1801—they got their wish. Italianastronomer Giuseppi Piazzi found a point of light moving at just the right speed to bethe desired planet, but it was just a dot, and too faint to physically be a terriblybig object. He suspected it might be a comet, but follow-up observations showed it wasn't.

The object was given the name Ceres... but was it really a planet?

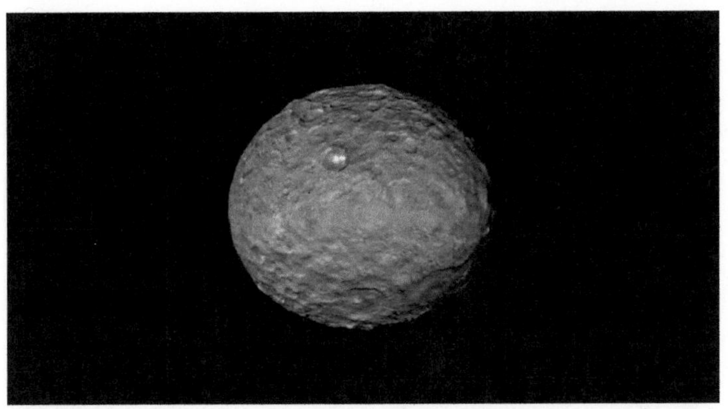

Ceres

Hopes were high that Ceres was the wished-for planet between Mars and Jupiter. But thensomething rather amazing happened: A little over a year later, in 1802, another one wasfound. Then, in 1804, astronomers spotted a third one, and a fourth in 1807.

It was becoming clear that a new class of solar system object had been discovered. Giventhat they were all just dots in the telescopes of the time, points of light like stars, theywere given the name "asteroids", which literally means star-like.

By the end of the 19th century more than 450 had been found in total. The rate of discoveryhas accelerated over the years, and now, today, we know of hundreds of thousands. There areprobably billions—yes, billions—of them larger than 100 meters across in the solarsystem, and over a million larger than 1 km in size.

So what are we dealing with here? What are these asteroids?

Asteroids

There's not really a hard-and-fast definition of what's an asteroid and what isn't.

But generally speaking, it's a class of smaller bodies that are rocky or metallicthat orbit the Sun out to Jupiter.

Objects past Jupiter have special designations.

Over the centuries we've learned a lot about them by scrutinizing them with telescopes.

Asteroids come in a few basic flavors. Most, of them, about 3/4, are carbonaceous, whichmeans they have lots of carbon in them. About 1/6th are silicaceous—heavy on the silicon-basedmaterials, y'know, rock. The rest are lumped into one catch-all category, but are dominatedby metallic objects, literally loaded with iron, nickel, and other metals.

So many of them orbit the Sun between Mars and Jupiter that this region is now calledthe Main Belt.

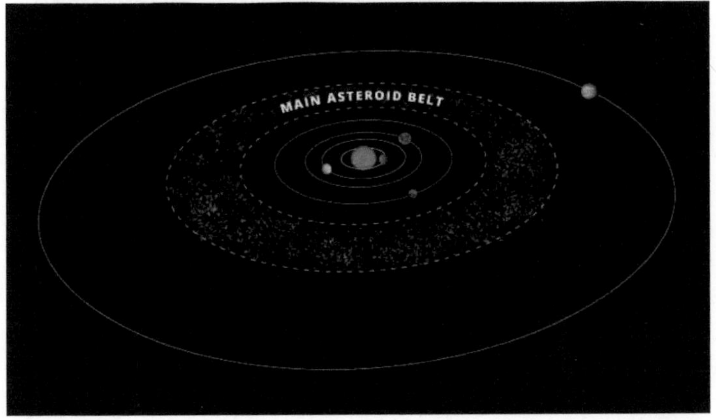

Asteroid Belt

The Main Belt has structure; for example, there are very few asteroidsabout 425 million kilometers from the Sun. An asteroid at that distance would have an orbital period of about 4 years; a simple fraction of Jupiter's 12 year period. Anyasteroid there would feel a repeated tug from Jupiter's mighty gravity, pulling it outof that orbit. The resulting gap is called the Kirkwood Gap, and there are several suchasteroid deserts, all with simple multiples of Jupiter's period. In this way, the mainbelt is like Saturn's rings, whose gaps are carved out by the gravity of the orbiting moons.

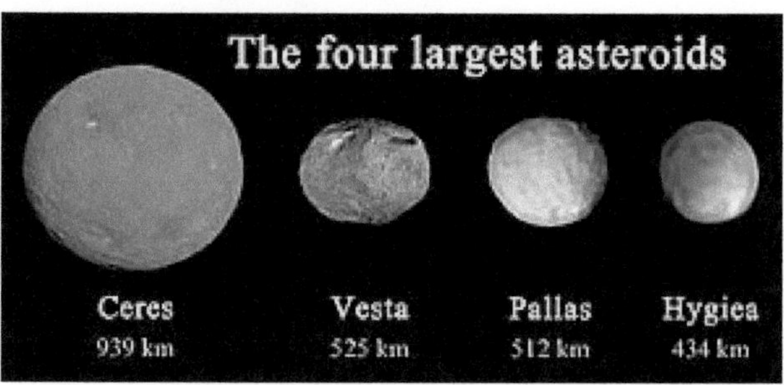

Another way to group asteroids is by orbit; some have similar orbits and may have formedfrom a bigger, parent asteroid that got disrupted by an impact. These groups are called families,and there are a few dozen known. For example, the Eunomia family has over 400 members, andare silicaceous, rocky asteroids and probably all formed from a parent body that was about 300 km across.

When you watch movies, they always show spaceships dodging and swooping through asteroid belts,trying to evade the bad guys. But in reality our asteroid belt is mostly empty space! Onaverage, decent-sized asteroids are millions of kilometers apart; so far that if you stoodon an asteroid, odds are good you wouldn't even be able to see another one with your naked eye.

And despite their huge numbers, they don't add up to much. If you took all the asteroidsin the main belt and lumped them together they'd be far smaller than our own

Moon!

Ceres is the biggest, at about 900 km across. It's round, nearly spherical due to itsown gravity crushing it into a ball.

Ceres was visited, by a spacecraft named Dawn . Ceres has a rocky core surrounded by a water ice mantle. The amount of water in it is staggering;probably more than all the fresh water on Earth! It may even be liquid under the surface, like the oceans of Enceladus and Europa.

Early images by Dawn as it approached the asteroid show its surface is heavily cratered,and some craters are very bright; they may be exposing ice under the surface, or justfresher, brighter material. There are tantalizing observations of localized water vapor on thesurface, which may be from sublimation; ice turning directly into a gas due to the Sun's heat, or it might indicate cryovolcanoes.

Dawn also visited Vesta, which is the third largest but second most massive asteroid known.

Vesta is round...ish, what's called an oblate spheroid, flattened a bit like a ball someone'ssitting on. The southern hemisphere got hammered by impacts long ago, leaving a huge basin there.

Several other main-belt asteroids have been visited by spacecraft, mostly via flybys.

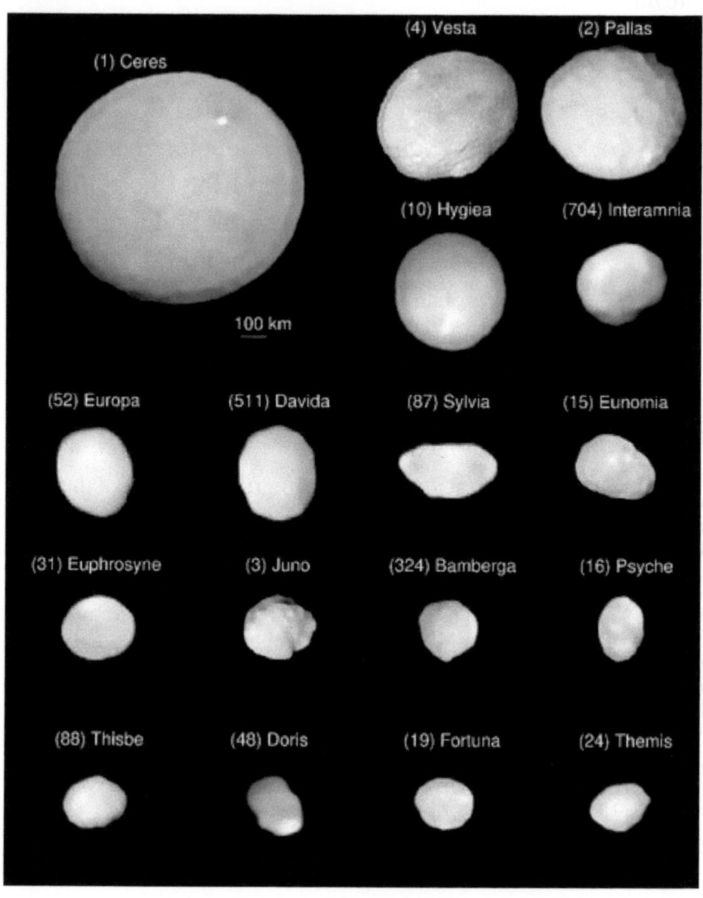

Lutetia, Gaspra, Steins, Mathilde. Ida is another, and was discovered to have a smallmoon orbiting it. In fact, a lot of asteroids have moons or are actually binary, with two similarly-sized bodies in orbit around each other. Kleopatra, a weird dog bone-shape rock, has two moons!

You might think asteroids are just giant versions of rocks you might find in your garden; tough,solid, singular bodies. But it turns out that's not the case. A few years ago scientists realisedthat asteroids have spent billions of years whacking into one another -- sometimes inhigh-speed collisions, sometimes more slowly. Slower hits can disrupt the asteroid, crack it,but not necessarily be strong enough to actually disrupt it so that it breaks apart.

Over time, enough hits like that can leave behind what's called a rubble pile: Individualrocks held together by their own gravity, like a bag of gravel, or a car window that's been cracked and still holds its overall shape.

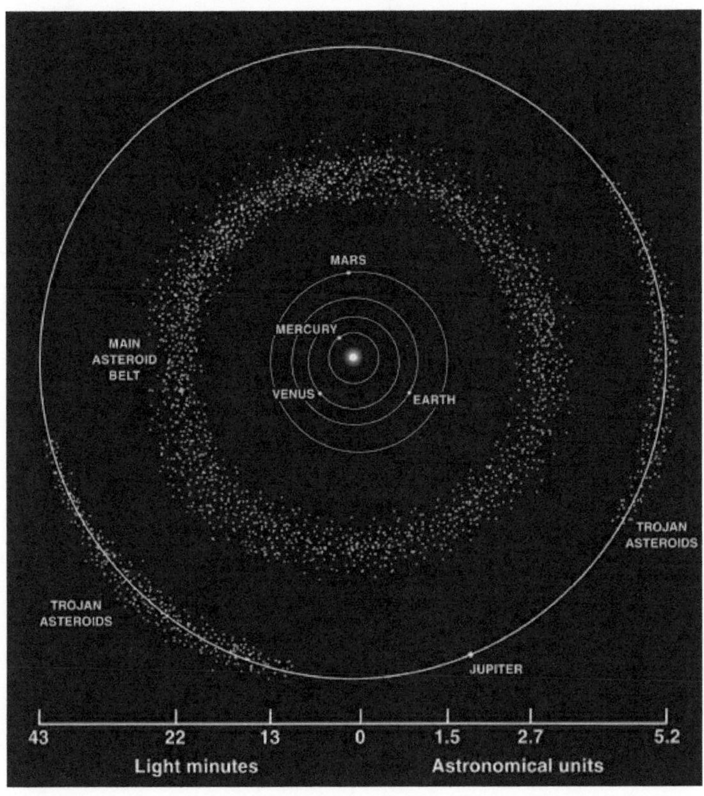

This became more clear when the Japanese Hayabusa spacecraft visited the asteroid Itokawa, and saw what can only be described as a jumbled mess. The asteroid had no craters on it, andwas littered with rubble and debris. It was also very low density, just what you'd expectfor a loosely bound rock pile.

It's weird to think of some asteroids as being not much more than free-floating bagsof gravel, but the Universe is under no obligation to adhere to our expectations. It's fullof surprises, and we need to keep our minds flexible.

So here's a question: why is there even a main asteroid belt at all?

The solar system formed from a disk of material, and over time, that material started to clumpinto bigger and bigger pieces. As planets formed, they swept up and pulled in lots morestuff, and grew large. Jupiter consumed a lot of the material around it, but not all,and left a lot of debris inside its orbit.

Some of this clumped together to form middling-sized objects, probably smaller than the planets we have now, but big enough to undergo differentiation: Heavy stuff like metals sank to the middle, and lighter stuff formed a mantle and crust. Collisions broke almost all of them apart,though, and that's why we see asteroids with different compositions: Some are fromthe denser core, others from the lighter crust.

There was probably a lot more material between Mars and Jupiter billions of years ago, butit either got eaten by Jupiter, or the planet's immense gravity altered the asteroids' orbits,flinging them away. This may be why Mars is so small, too; Jupiter robbed it of all ofits food as it formed.

While most asteroids live in the main belt, not all of them do. Some have orbits thatcross that of Mars, taking them closer to the Sun. We call those --Mars-crossingasteroids. Some have orbits that take them even closer to the Sun, crossing Earth'sorbit. We call those... Apollo asteroids.They're named after the asteroidApollo, the first of its kind to be found.

Some have orbits that are already entirely inside Earth's orbit, called Aten asteroids.

Aten and Apollo asteroids can get pretty close to Earth, so we call them Near-Earth Asteroids.

Now, while they get close to us, that doesn't mean they'll hit us, because, for example,their orbits may be tilted, so their orbits and the orbit of the Earth don't actually ever physically cross.

But... some do have paths that literally intersect Earth's. That doesn't mean they'll hitus every pass, either; after all, you can walk across a street without getting hit bya car. The problem comes when you try to occupy the same volume of space as a car at the same time.

Astronomers, unsurprisingly, are very concerned about asteroids that can hit us. That'swhy we have surveys, observatories scanning the skies, looking for them.

Asteroid Belt

There's another category of asteroid that exists due to a quirk of gravity. When a planetorbits a star, there are points along the planet's orbit and near it in space wherethe gravitational forces are in balance. If you place an object there, it tends to staythere, like an egg in a cup. These are called Lagrange points. One of them is along thesame orbit as the planet, but 60° ahead; another is 60° behind.

The first such asteroid found was orbiting 60° ahead Jupiter, and was named Achilles,after the Greek hero in the Trojan war. As more were found, the naming convention stuck;asteroids ahead of Jupiter were named after Greek figures in the Trojan war, and those behind Jupiter were named for Trojans, and now we just call them all Trojan asteroids.

Trojan asteroids have been spotted for Jupiter, Mars, Uranus, Neptune, and even Earth! Earth's was found in 2010 using observations by an orbiting observatory called WISE, which scansthe skies in infrared light, where asteroids glow due to their own heat. 2010 TK7, as it's called, is about 300 meters across and 800 million kilometers away, orbiting the Sun ahead of the Earth.

There are also asteroids that have orbits that are very similar to Earth's, but areslightly elliptical and tilted with respect to ours. Because of this, they can stay relativelynear the Earth in space, but don't really orbit us; instead they sometimes get closerand sometimes recede. It's pretty weird, but a natural outcome of orbital mechanics.

Some people say these asteroids are moons of Earth, but it's better to say they'reco-orbital with us. Only a few are known, the most famous being Cruithne, which can get as close as 12 or so million kilometers from us.

Originally, asteroids were named after female goddesses; Ceres, Vesta, Juno, and so on. But as hundreds more were found, and then thousands, we ran outof names. Eventually astronomers who discovered asteroids were allowed to name them -- through a lengthy proposal and acceptance process governed by the International Astronomical Union. They also get a number assigned to them as well.

Asteroids and Pluto

A lot of astronomers have asteroids named after them, including astronomers who study asteroids, like Eleanor Helin, who discovered quite a few asteroids and comets. Hers is3267 Glo; for her nickname.

CHAPTER TWENTY-ONE

THE COMETS

Comet

Since humans have been human we've looked to the skies forportents of the future.

The Sun, the Moon, the planets, the stars; they've all been used for prognostication.And so have comets.

A fuzzy blob, moving slowly across the stars? How could soothsayersresist?

But now we know a lot more about comets.

They're beautiful, fascinating, and can bring both life and death upon our little world.Comets have been seen the sky since antiquity.

Comet Halley, for example, is shown in the Bayeux Tapestry, which depicts the Normaninvasion of the British Isles in the year 1066.

It was seen by ancient Chinese and Greeks, too.

In general, and like everything else in the sky, comets were considered omens orharbingers of human events.Sometimes they were good omens,William the Conqueror liked his chances in 1066 after seeing one

and sometimes bad ,that same comet didn't do so well for King Harold II.

A comet bright enough to see with the naked eye shows up in the heavensevery few years or so, and some can get spectacularly bright.

When you think of a comet, you probably picture a fuzzy blob and a long tail stretching away from it.

Fair enough. But there's a bit more to them than that.

Comets are in many ways similar to asteroids.

They're roughly hewn chunks of stuff left over from the formation of the solar system.Unlike asteroids, which are mostly rock with a dash of ice and maybe metal,comets are a more balanced mixture of ice and rock.

And by "ice" I mean frozen water -- but also frozen carbon dioxide, carbon monoxide,methane, ammonia - things we normally think of as gases on Earth.

And by "rock" I do mean rocks, but also gravel and dust.

In fact, astronomers sometimes call comets "dirty snowballs," which isn't a half-bad term.It's that ice that makes comets, well, comets.

When they're way out in deep space they're so cold that they're basically inert lumps of ice and rock.But many are on elliptical orbits that take them from those sub-freezingdepths into our neck of the woods, where the Sun can warm them.As they heat up the ice turns directly into a gas — a process called "sublimation."

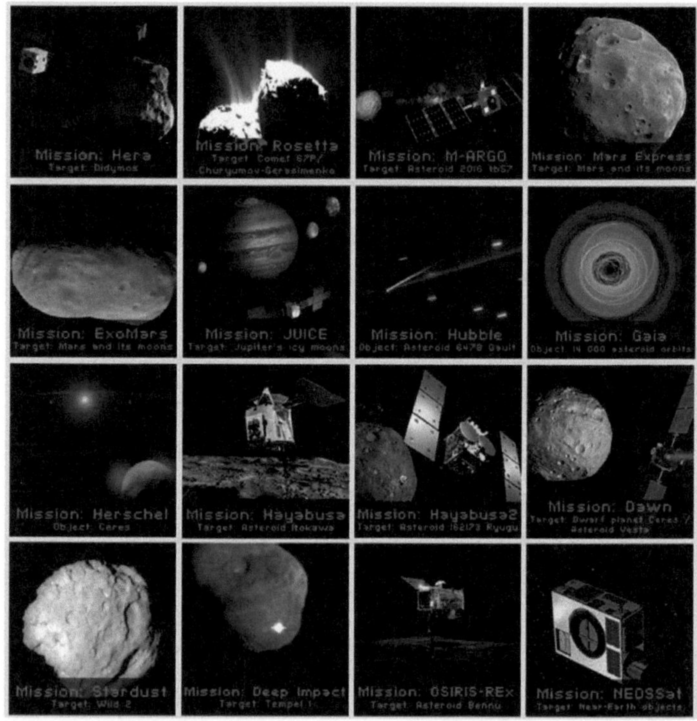

The gas then flows away from the comet, creating a cloud around it.

This makes the comet look fuzzy, and actually in the past they've been called "hairy stars."

I like that term too, and in a sense we still use it.

The solid part of the comet is called the nucleus, and the gaseous cloud around it iscalled the coma — Latin for "hair." In fact, that's why we called them "comets."

As the ice sublimates, the bits of rock and gravel and dust embedded in it can be freedand leave the nucleus as well.

This material is what forms the comet's tail, but how that happens depends on whichmaterial you're talking about.

The gas and the dust from comets form two different tails.

Gas molecules emitted by the comet get ionised by the Sun's ultraviolet light.That means they lose electrons, becoming charged,and charged particles are highly susceptible to magnetic fields.

The solar wind is a stream of charged particles blown out by the Sun, and carries a magnetic field with it.

As the wind hits the ionized gas from the comet, it picks up those particlesand carries them downstream, away from the Sun.

The solar wind is usually moving far, far faster thanthe comet, so this "ion tail" winds up pointing directly away from the Sun.

The dust, on the other hand, is influenced more by sunlight.

Light from the Sun exerts a small but inexorable pressure, and this pushes on the dust particles.

The dust streams away, but because the pressure isn't as intense as the solar wind is on the gas tail,the dust tail blows away more lazily, and tends to lag behind the comet in its orbit.

Several nations sent spacecraft to fly past the comet, and the Soviet mission Vega 1was the first to successfully get pictures of the nucleus. The low-resolution images revealeda dark lump highlighted with two bright spots, later determined to be jets of gas streaming away.

These images were used to better determine the position of the nucleus,and a few days later the European probe Giotto zipped past the nucleusat an incredibly close distance of just 600 kilometers.

Those pictures were more detailed, and showed us a flying mountain, an irregular chunk 15 x 8 kilometers in size.

And it was dark, reflecting only 4% of the light that hit it.

That makes the nucleus as black as asphalt!

You might think that all that ice would be shiny, but it's not that simple.

Most of Halley's nucleus is covered in thick dust laced with darker molecules,with only a few spots emitting gas. Most likely, there are deposits of ice under the surface,and only some of them receive enough heat from the Sun to sublimate and blow out gas.

This has been seen with other comets as well, the gas is emitted from specific spots on the comet, venting out from cracks in the crusty surface.

The surfaces of comets must be inhomogeneous, different in different places.

That fact was brought home magnificently in 2014 by another European mission, Rosetta.

It went into orbit around the comet 67P/Churyumov-Gerasimenko, and found it to be a bizarre little object.

Measuring about 4 kilometers end-to-end, 67P has two lobesconnected by a narrow neck, looking very much like a cosmic rubber ducky.

The surface is completely devoid of craters; clearly the surface is very young.Images show jets of gas emitted from very specific places on the surface,and there are wide circular pits here and there which may be gas vents,growing wider over time as the ice below is depleted.

Surprisingly, the surface is fairly tough and hard, when some scientists expected it to be fluffier.

The comet has a very low density, similar to rubble-pile asteroids, so it was expected that the surface would be soft.

Rosetta sent down a lander named Philae to set down on the surface, using harpoons to anchor itself,

but instead the lander bounced, unable to penetrate the tougher-than-expected material.

One idea to explain this is that the ice is porous and fluffier inside the comet,but as it nears the Sun the ice at the surface warms and changes its structure, forming that harder crust.

As for the double-lobed thing, well that's a bit baffling. We see some asteroids shaped that way as well.

It's possible 67P used to be two separate comets that had a low speed collision and stuck together.

Or maybe it used to be one big lump, but over the eons the ice in the middle sublimatedmore, leaving behind the two lobes.

Rosetta is the first time in human history we've had a probe orbiting a comet,studying it up close and long-term. We're still learning, still figuring this stuff out.

Incidentally, I mentioned earlier that ,comets have lots of ice in them and they also get really close to Earth sometimes.

In fact, they can hit us!billions of years ago lots of comets hit the Earth not long after our planet formed.

Together with asteroids — many of which are also rich in water ice — they may have brought a significant amount of water to Earth! Scientists are still wrestlingover the details of this,and it may be a while before the actual numbers are nailed down, but it's an intriguing thought.

Even more interesting? In 2004, NASA's Stardust space probe physically passed throughthe coma of comet Wild 2, collecting samples that were returned to Earth.

Careful analysis of the material found the presence of organic, carbon based molecules in them.

And not just any random molecules, but complex ones, including amino acids!

These are the building blocks of all life on Earth; amino acids are what our bodies use to create proteins.

It's possible that the ingredients of life on Earth didn't start here, but instead were brought toour planet from comet impacts. Or, at least, there was a mix of the two.

If that's the case, then in a sense, all life on Earth is part alien. How about that?

But what gets me are thephilosophical ramifications of this. When we look into space,when we examine our celestial neighbours, when we send probes to comets and survey what we find,we're looking at our own origins. Comets are like time machines, allowing us to investigate our past,four billion years back, hinting at the secrets of the origin of life itself.

And you thought astronomy was just lying out in a field and looking up.

Well, it is, but if you let it, it's also a whole lot more.

METEOR TERMINOLOGY
AMERICAN METEOR SOCIETY - WWW.AMSMETEORS.ORG
COMET
A solid body made of ice, rock, dust and frozen gases. As they fracture and disintegrate, some comets leave a trail of solid debris.
Nucleus (solid part): tens of kilometers.
Tail: millions of kilometers.
ASTEROID
Small rocky, iron or icy debris flying in space.
From 1 meter to hundreds of kilometers.
METEOROID
A small asteroid.
From microns to 1 meter.
METEOR SHOWER
An annual event, when the Earth passes through a region having a great concentration of debris, such as particles left by a comet. From Earth, it looks like meteors radiate from the same point in the night sky.
METEOR
The light emitted from a meteoroid or an asteroid as it enters the atmosphere.
FIREBALL
A meteor brighter than the planet Venus.
BOLIDE
The light emitted by a large meteoroid or an asteroid as it explodes in the atmosphere.
METEORITE
A fragment of a meteoroid or an asteroid that survives passage through the atmosphere and hits the ground.
From few grams to several dozen of tonnes.
AMS

CHAPTER TWENTY-TWO

THE OORT CLOUD

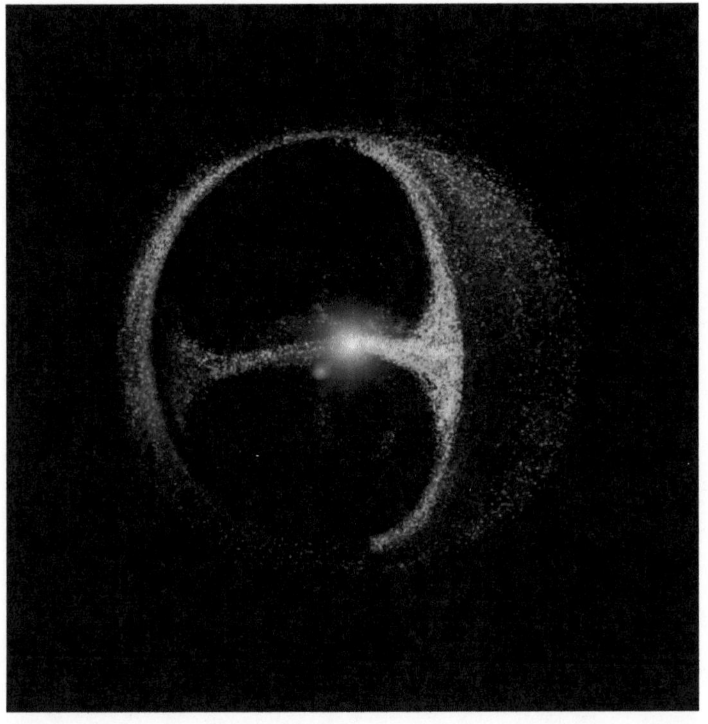

The Oort Cloud

Well, look where we are now. With our backs to the Sun, and the planets, asteroids, andcomets behind us, we face deep space. There's nothing between us and the stars, so terriblyterribly far away.... or is there?

The empty space past Neptune isn't exactly empty. I earlier mentioned that cometscome in two varieties: Those with orbital periods of less than 200 years, which tendto orbit the Sun in the same plane as the planets, and those with longer periods, whichhave orbits tilted every which-way.This is something of a problem: Comets lose material when they get near the Sun. Overthe course of millions of years these comets should evaporate! And yet here we are, 4.56billion years after the solar system's birth, and comets still appear in our skies.

So, where are they coming from?

To see, we'll have to turn the clock back a wee bit - like, 4.5 billion years.

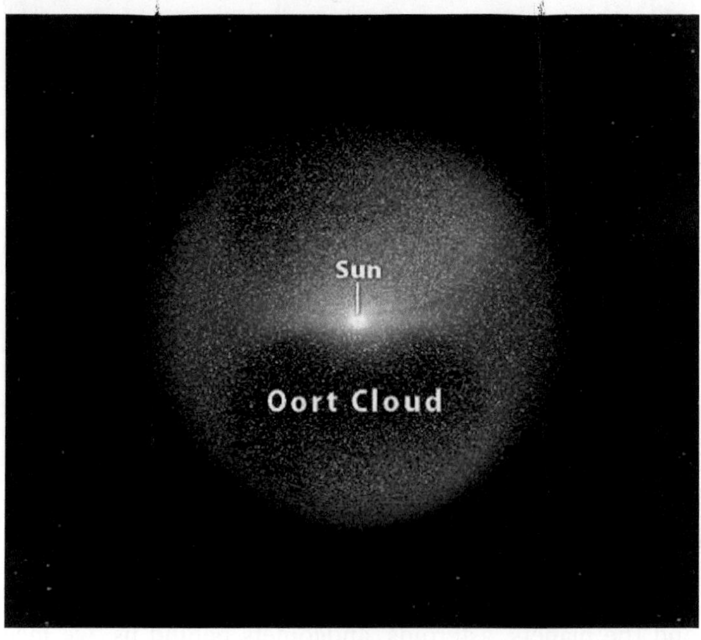

Behold, our forming solar system. Coalescing out of a flat disk of material around theSun, the inner planets were warmer, smaller, and rocky, while the outer planets were ina region that was colder, and grew huge. Out there in the chillier part of the solar system,water came in the form of ice mixed in with dust and other stuff. These bits would collideand stick together, growing bigger. Some grew to hundreds ofkilometers across.

But there was a problem: those outer planets. They had a lot of gravity, and any chunk ofice getting too close would either fall into the planet and get assimilated or get kickedinto a different orbit. It could then plunge in toward the Sun, or get flung out into deep space.

Trillions upon trillions of such iceballs got tossed around by the planets. Even thoughthey were small compared to the planets, they did have a little bit of mass and gravity,so every time the planet pulled hard on them, they also pulled a little bit on the planets,too. It wasn't much per chunk, but after trillions of events this adds up! A currentmodel of what happened, called the Nice model after the city in France where it was proposed,says that the overall effect of all these encounters was that Saturn, Uranus, and Neptuneslowly moved outward from the Sun, while Jupiter moved inward.

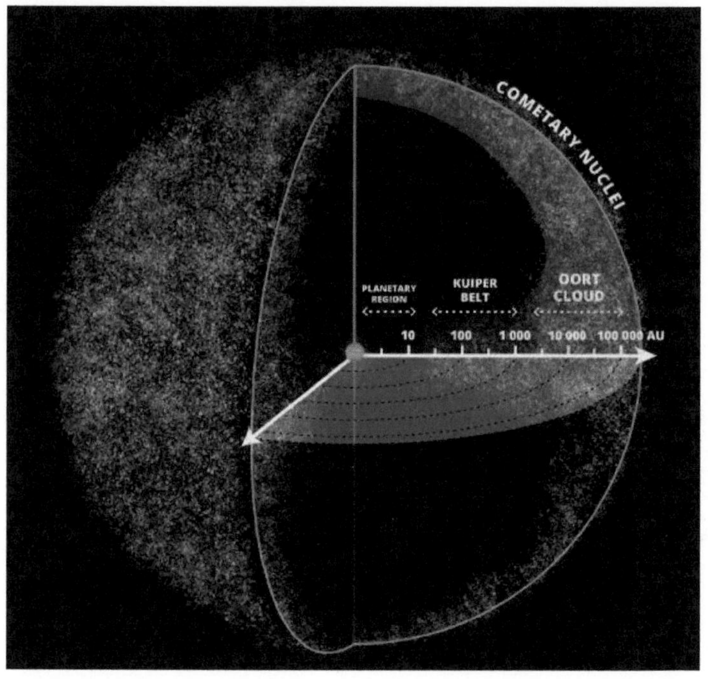

Neptune would have had the biggest effect on these iceballs, because it bordered thebiggest volume of space where they lived. As Neptune migrated outward, close encounterswith these chunks of ice flung lots of them into crazy orbits, highlyelliptical and tiltedwith respect to the planets. Repeated more distant encounters tended to more slowly increasethe sizes of the orbits of the iceballs, too.

We think that this shuffling around of the outer planets is what caused the Late HeavyBombardment, the intense shower of objects that came screaming down from the outer solarsystem, scarring planets and moons, a few hundred million years after the planets themselvesformed.

It's not known for sure, but all the pieces fit together really well.

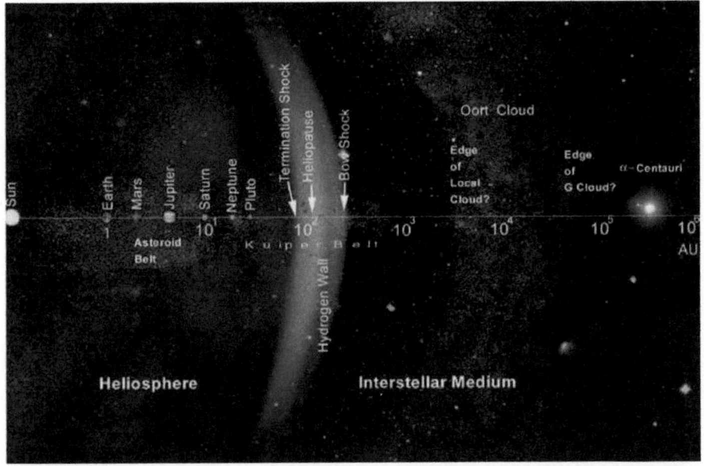

In the end, there are three rather distinct populations of these objects. One is a regionshaped like a puffy disk or a doughnut, aligned with the plane of the planets. Icy objectsthere have stable orbits, unaffected by Neptune. We call this the Kuiper Belt, named afterthe Dutch astronomer Gerard Kuiper, one of many who initially speculated about the existenceof this region. The Kuiper Belt starts more or less just outside Neptune's orbit, extendingfrom about 4.5 to 7.5 billion kilometers from the Sun.

The second region is called the scattered disk. This is composed of the iceballs sentby Neptune into those weird, highly tilted orbits. This overlaps the Kuiper Belt on its inner edge, and extends out to perhaps 150 billion kilometers from the Sun—that's25 times farther out than Neptune.

Finally, outside those two zones there's a spherical cloud of icy objects which startsroughly 300 billion kilometers out— 70 times farther out than Neptune, a staggering 2000times the distance of the Earth from the Sun. And that's just where it starts: It extendsway farther out than that, perhaps as much as a light year, 10 trillion kilometers! Thisis called the Oort Cloud, after astronomer Jan Oort who first proposed it.

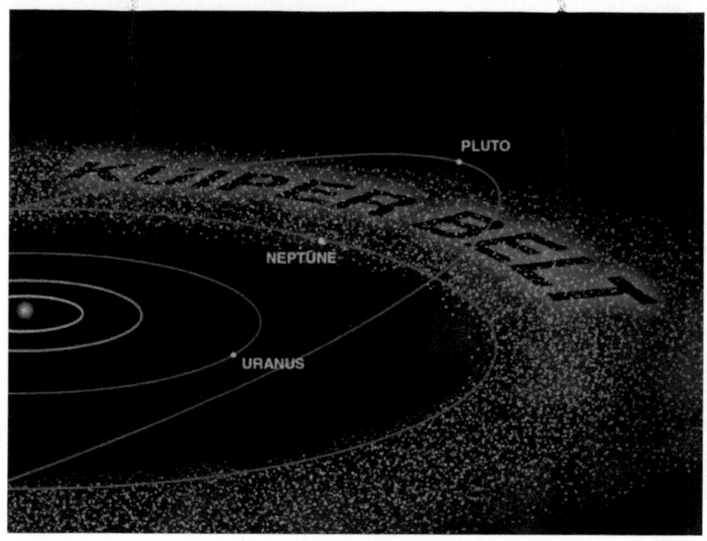

Kuiper belt

The Oort Cloud is the origin of long period comets. Since they orbit the Sun on a spherewith no preferred orientation, they come in toward the inner solar system from randomdirections in the sky. Many newly discovered comets fall into this category. Their orbitscan be extremely long; they start their fall from so far away they swing around the Sunat nearly escape velocity, and their orbits are close to being parabolic.

The scattered disk is the source of short period comets. They can still be affectedby Neptune, which can alter their orbits to drop them down closer in. They can orbit theSun on paths between Jupiter and Neptune, meaning eventually they'll have a closeencounter with Jupiter. This can send them in closer to the Sun, and they become short period comets.

That's how comets are made.

So how do we know all this? Well, until 1930 it was pretty much just conjecture. But thenan American astronomer, Clyde Tombaugh, discovered the first Kuiper Belt Object: Pluto.

Pluto orbits the Sun on an elliptical, mildly-tilted path. Its orbit actually brings it closerto the Sun than Neptune! So how come it never collides with the larger planet?

Pluto's orbit crosses Neptune's...more or less. Because the orbit is tilted, theynever actually physically cross. When Pluto is at perihelion, closest to the Sun, it'swell above the plane of the solar system, far from Neptune's orbit.

Not only that, but Pluto orbits the Sun twice for every three times Neptune does. Becauseof this, whenever Pluto is closest to the Sun, Neptune is always 90° away in its orbit.

That's many billions of kilometers distant, way too far to affect Pluto.

This is mostly coincidence. We've seen how orbital resonances can be forced by tidesand by gravity. But in this case it's due to attrition. Once upon a time, billions ofyears ago, there were probably a lot of objects out by Pluto, with orbits of all different shapes and tilts.

But the ones that got too close to Neptune got gravitationally tweaked into differentorbits, turning them into comets or flinging them deeper into space. The only ones thatcould survive just happened to have orbits with that 3:2 or 2:1 resonance with Neptune,keeping them far from Neptune's influence. Today, those are the only kinds of objectswe see with orbits near Neptune.

We call these objects plutinos. They're not really a separate class of object—they'restill Kuiper Belt objects, but a fun and interesting subset of them.

Once Pluto was found, astronomers wondered if it might herald a new class of icy objectspast Neptune. However, it took more than six decades to find the next one! 1992 QB1 wasdiscovered in 1992, and that opened a sort of gold rush of Kuiper Belt discoveries. Wenow know of more than a thousand Kuiper Belt Objects. One, called Eris, is very close toPluto's size and is more massive — it's probably rockier than icy Pluto.

Pluto is an interesting object. A moon was discovered in 1978. Named Charon, it's actually about $1/8^{th}$ the mass of Pluto itself! While Charon orbits Pluto, the moon has enough massthat it can be said that Pluto noticeably orbits Charon, too. In reality, both circlearound their mutual centre of mass, located between the two.

Four more moons were discovered in Hubble images of Pluto in 2005 and 2012. There maybe more. Pluto is so small and distant that we don't know much about it... but that may be about to change.

Pluto was found in 1930, long before any other KuiperBelt Object, because it's much brighter than any other. When it was discovered, itwas thought to be about the size of Earth. But over the years better observations showedit to be far smaller than first thought; in fact it's smaller than Earth's Moon! Itssurface is unusually reflective, shiny, making it look much bigger than it seems. Most otherKuiper Belt denizens are far less reflective, and so are far fainter.

If Pluto is King of the Kuiper Belt Objects, it has a lot of loyal subjects. We think theKuiper Belt may have 100,000 objects in it larger than 100 km wide. If that sounds like a lot, get this: The Oort Cloud, surrounding the solar system, may have trillions of icy bodies in it. Trillions!

While we know of lots of Kuiper Belt Objects, we don't know of any Oort Cloud objectsfor sure. Two very interesting bodies have been found: Sedna, and VP113. Sedna's orbittakes it an incredible 140 billion km from the Sun, while VP113 gets about half thatfar out. Both are on very elliptical orbits. Neither, however, gets close to Neptune, soit's not at all clear how they got where they are. They may be Oort Cloud objects thatwere disturbed by passing stars long ago, dropping them closer into the Sun. But no one knows. Yet.Speaking of which... we can calculate how many Oort Cloud objects there should be leftover from the formation of the solar system, and it's about 6 billion. However, calculatinghow many there are using long period comet observations, you wind up getting about 400billion. That's a big discrepancy! Now get this: One idea to solve this discrepancy is that the Sun has stolen comets from other stars. Seriously! Comets should form whereverstars do, and sometimes the Sun passes near other stars. When we see a long-period cometgracing our skies, could we be seeing an object from an alien solar system? Maybe.

There is another explanation, but it's highly speculative. Perhaps there's another planetin the solar system, well beyond Neptune.

It's possible. Some very preliminary studies have shown that some long-period comets aren'tcoming in randomly, but instead have their orbits aligned in a way you might expect ifa very distant planet perturbed them. There are a handful of Kuiper Belt Objects aligned in a similar way.

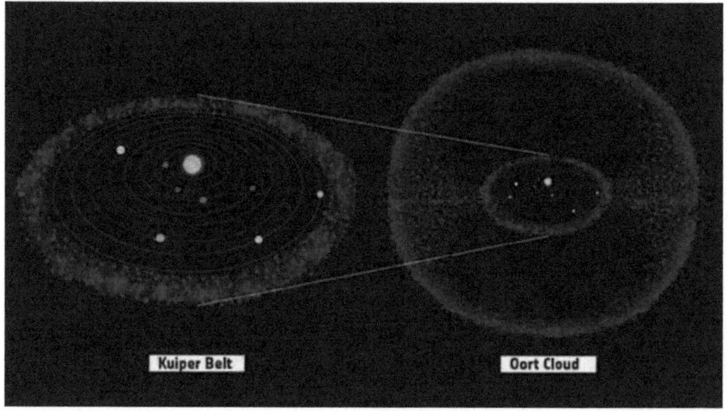

NASA's WISE observatory scanned the skies in infrared, and would've seen anythingas big as Jupiter or Saturn out to tremendous distances, so any hypothetical planet wouldhave to be smaller. And very distant, probably tens of billions of kilometers out. We'veseen other stars with planets this far out, so it's physically possible.

But is there one really there? We can't say either way, yes or no. At least, not yet.

This region of the solar system is seriously underexplored. It's distant, difficult toreach, and above all else extremely huge and numbingly empty. You could hide a whole planetout there, and it would be pretty hard to find.

The point? There's still lots of solar system left to explore. We've barely dipped ourtoes into these dark, frigid waters.

CHAPTER TWENTY-THREE

THE METEOR

A Meteor

I love astronomy. You may have noticed. But there's one reallyfrustrating aspect ofit: Everything westudy is really far away.

Nearly everything we understand about the Universe comes from light emitted or reflectedby objects. It'd be nice if we could get actual samples from them; physical specimens we could examine in the lab.

If you go outside on a clear, dark, moonless night, and you really should chancesare pretty good that within a few minutes you'll see a shooting star.

A Shooting Star

It'll zipacross the sky, a fiery dot leaving a long glowing trail behind it. They're one ofthe most exciting and fun things you'll seewhen you look up, and they always geta gasp and a squeal of delight from people someone who's stargazing.

What you're actually seeing is a tiny bit of interplanetary debris: rock, ice, or metalramming through the Earth's atmosphere, heated toincandescence. Most are faint, butsome can be astonishingly bright.

Obviously, shooting stars aren't really stars. So what do we call them?

Sometimes it seems like astronomers use different names for objects to keep things as confusingas possible. But really, they do that to separate out different things. In this case, the actualbit of solid stuff coming from space is called a meteoroid.

The phenomenon of the meteoroid getting hot and blazing across the sky is called a meteor.

And finally, if it hits the ground, we call it a meteorite.

I think the best way to tick off an astronomer is to mix up meteor and meteorite.

Sometimes astronomers can be pretty pedantic about such things.

Amazingly, a typical meteor that you'll see is due to a meteoroid that's tiny, probablysmaller than a grain of sand! How can that be?

It's because they're hauling mass.

The meteoroid is orbiting the Sun, probably at speeds of a few dozen kilometers per second.As it approaches the Earth, our planet's gravity accelerates it an additional 11 kilometersper second — Earth's escape velocity. And when it enters our atmosphere it's movingincredibly fast, up to 70 km/sec or more.

Meteors

The energy of motion is called kinetic energy. If you want to get something moving, you haveto give it energy, and if you want it to stop, you have to take that energy away. This kineticenergy depends on the mass of the object and how fast it's moving. In fact, it dependson the square of the velocity; double its speed and it'll have four times the kineticenergy.

Meteoroids may usually be small, but they're screaming fast, and have a huge amount ofkinetic energy. As they hit our atmosphere they slow from their ridiculous orbital speedto nearly a standstill, and all that energy has to go somewhere. It gets converted intolight and heat, and that's what we see as a meteor.

A big misconception about meteors is that they get hot due to friction with air. Actually,a far bigger contributor to their heat is compression. One of the most basic laws ofphysics is that when you compress a gas it heats up. And a meteoroid coming in at hypersonicspeeds compresses the air in front of it a lot, heating it hugely. The gas can reach temperatures of thousands of degrees Celsius for a few seconds.

The air radiates away this heat, in turn heating up the meteoroid. The material on the surfacevaporises and blows away—a process called ablation. That ablated material leaves a glowingtrail behind the meteor, which we call a train. Sometimes it can glow for several minutes,getting twisted up in high altitude winds, leaving behind an eerie, ghost-like persistent train. This all happens high above your head, about 90 – 100 km above the ground.

Typically, from any one location, you can see a few meteors per hour. It may not seemlike much, but when you add them up all over the planet you find the Earth is getting peltedto the tune of about 100 tons of material a day. But again, most of these meteoroidsare teeny tiny.

Those random meteors are called sporadic meteors. They tend to be rocky in composition, andgenerally come from asteroids. If two asteroids smack into each other, the collision can ejectlittle bits of material that then orbit the Sun on their own. If their orbit crosses theEarth, then you have a potential meteor. It may take a few million years, but at somepoint the Earth and the meteoroid are at the same place at the same time, and boom.

But sometimes meteoroids travel in packs. When that happens, we can get meteor showers , many dozens or even hundreds of meteors per hour. With one exception, those don't comefrom asteroids: They come from comets.

When a comet orbits the Sun, the ice on it turns to gas, dislodging dust and gravel mixedin. This material leaves the comet and tends to stay more or less in the same orbit asthe comet itself. Over time, that material gets scattered all along the orbit, creating a puffy ribbon of tiny pieces of space debris around the Sun.

When the Earth plows through that cloud of debris, we get a meteor shower.

From our viewpoint on Earth we see meteors shooting across the sky, apparently radiatingaway from a single point. That's a perspective effect; it's like driving through a tunneland seeing the tiles on the wall and ceiling flying past you, all apparently coming from a point ahead of you. The point in the sky where the meteors come from is called theradiant, and the shower is named after the constellation the radiant's in. So we havethe Perseid meteor shower, the Leonids, the Camelo pardalids.

And, since the Earth hits a specific comet stream around the same time every year, theshowers are annual. The Perseids are in August, and the Leonids in November.

Perseids

Watching a meteor shower is easy: Just go outside and look up! Generally, they'rebetter after local midnight. The Earth plows into the meteoroids, so facing the direction of Earth's orbital motion means more meteors, just like you get more raindrops on the frontwindshield of your car than than on the back when driving through a storm. After localmidnight you're on the part of the Earth facing into the orbit, so you see more meteors.

By the way, if you happen to be on the International Space Station, you have to look down to seea meteor. In 2011, astronaut Ron Garan photographed a Perseid burning up below him! But don'tworry: The odds of the Space Station getting hit are extremely low. Space is big.

Geminids

Oh, and that one exception I mentioned before? That's the annual Geminids shower, which occurs in December. That comes from the asteroid 3200 Phaethon, which is on an orbit that takes it very close to the Sun. It's possible it gets so hot that the rock vaporises, makingit act like a comet.

The vast majority of meteoroids are small and tend to burn up in our atmosphere. Butthey can be bigger. A bolide, or fireball, is an extremely bright meteor, and those canbe about the size of a grapefruit. Those happen pretty often somewhere over the Earth.

Very rarely, an incoming meteoroid will survive all the way to the ground and become a meteorite.

Sometimes, the immense pressure of ramming Earth's air causes the incoming meteoroidto crumble or even explode, raining down dozens or hundreds of smaller pieces. Typically,they slow rapidly after their blaze of glory, and simply fall the rest of the way to theground. The air up there is cold, and their interiors are cold from being in space solong. So, despite what you might think, meteorites don't cause fires when they hit the ground.

In fact, they can be quite chilly!

Meteorites are classified into three broad categories: Stony, which are mostly rock;iron, which are mostly metal; and stony iron, which are a mixture of the two. The majority of meteorites we find are stony.

The stony meteorites are subdivided into two kinds: Chondrites, and achondrites. Chondritescontain chondrules, small grains of minerals. These are very primitive, and are thoughtto have condensed out of the original disk of material that formed the solar system.Their age can be found by looking at ratios of elements in them formed from radioactivedecay. The oldest known meteorite formed 4.568 billion years ago: Before the Earth itself formed!

Achondrites don't have chondrules in them. Most likely they came from a bigger asteroid,one that was once molten through, mixing the minerals. A big collision disrupted the parentbody, creating the achondritic meteoroids.

Iron meteorites most likely come from the center of a large asteroid, one big enoughthat metals fell to the center via gravity. Again, a big impact blew the asteroid up,scattering its material around the asteroid belt, and with some on orbits that eventuallyintersected Earth.

Stony irons are the rarest. Some have green or orange crystals of a mineral called olivineembedded in a web of metal. Called pallasites, they may be the most beautiful of all meteorites.

Of course, on occasion the meteoroid coming in can be a tad bigger. And when that happens, well, all hell can break loose.

On February 15, 2013, residents of the Russian city of Chelyabinsk got a rude awakening.

At 9:20 a.m. local time, a rock about 19 meters across came in at a low angle. It got nearlyas bright as the Sun as it slammed into theatmosphere, and the pressure of its passagebroke it up into several chunks, which broke up again. In a moment's time, the suddenenergy released was equivalent to the detonation of a half million tons of TNT — as muchas a small atomic bomb!

While no one was killed, over a thousand people were injured by flying glass, shattered bythe explosion. No doubt they were at their windows gawking at the huge vapor trail inthe sky when the shock wave hit.

There was no warning for this event; the asteroid was essentially too small to detect whileit was out in space. Well, for now at least. Telescopes are coming online soon that shouldbe able to find smaller asteroids and give us some warning. Astronomers are more worried about ones roughly a hundred meters across or bigger; these can do serious damage on a city-wide scale or larger, but at the moment aren't easy to spot much in advance.

Meteor Hitting Earth

And what do we do if we do see one headed our way? As of right now, there's not muchwe can do.

Studies have been done to determine the best course of action; maybe lobbing anuke at it, or simply ramming it with a space probe to change the orbit and make sure it misses Earth. These ideas look good on paper, but they haven't been tested yet. We're stilla few years from that.

The good news is that objects that size hitting the Earth are rare; maybe once every centuryor three. But if we do nothing, it will happeneventually. As science fiction writer Larry Niven points out, the dinosaurs went extinct because they didn't have a space program.

Hopefully, we're smarter than they were.

9 798887 493879

Printed by Libri Plureos GmbH in Hamburg, Germany